FERRY & CRUISE SHIP

annual

2010

ИВАН ФРАНКО

Published by:
Ferry Publications, PO Box 33, Ramsey, Isle of Man IM99 4LP
Tel: +44 (0) 1624 898446 Fax: +44 (0) 1624 898449
E-mail: ferrypubs@manx.net Website: www.ferrypubs.co.uk

FERRY
Publications

CONTENTS

1 Farewell to the *SeaFrance Renoir* 4

2 Photo Feature - Liverpool 14

3 Cruising the Red Sea 24

4 Photo Feature - Small Ferries 32

5 Holyhead Routes to Dublin Bay 42

6 Changes to the Isle of Wight Routes 54

7 Photo Feature - Ostend & Zeebrugge 63

8 Notable Cruise Ship Withdrawals 76

9 Harwich International Cruise Port 86

10 Soviet Russia's 'Author' Class 90

11 Photo Feature - Dover Cruise Ships 95

12 Crossing the Adriatic 106

INTRODUCTION

Following the great success of Ferry Publications' first 'Ferry & Cruise Annual' last year, we now offer our readers a new edition for 2010. The feedback from the 2009 annual was extremely positive and we greatly appreciate the many encouraging comments that were made concerning its content and presentation.

Ever since founding Ferry Publications in 1987, we have always sought to provide our readers with high quality photographic images and outstanding reproduction. The advent of digital photography has undoubtedly allowed a growing number of people to supply us with high-resolution photographs that they are happy to share with a greater audience and we very much hope that this will continue.

The successful formula with a book such as this is to provide a series of ferry and cruise ship articles dealing with not only present day activities but also to afford an opportunity to share a retrospective glimpse into the recent past. Like it or not, change is an inevitable feature of our lives and this is especially the case for those of us who follow the ferry and cruise ship fleets. The majority of our articles in the 2010 annual reflect change of one sort or another: changes to ports and their traffic, to historic routes and to elderly ships that have recently been withdrawn from service.

We are already thinking ahead to the 2011 annual and should any of our readers have any thoughts or suggestions concerning it, we would naturally be delighted to hear from them.

Miles Cowsill & John Hendy
October 2009

The best of modern ferry design demonstrated by the **Superfast XI** *making an evening departure from Igoumenitsa on her way from Patras to Ancona. (John May)*

1 Farewell to the *SeaFrance Renoir*
by John Hendy

The passing of the veteran French vehicle ferry *SeaFrance Renoir* in May 2009, very much ended an era on the Dover Strait.

THE SCENE IS SET

The nationalised French railway company, SNCF, entered the car ferry trade much later than its British counterparts and the *Compiegne* of 1958 was their very first such vessel to be constructed. Built at Rouen, the new ship was essentially a seasonal carrier of tourist cars and vied for traffic on the Dover–Calais route with the diminutive Townsend ferry *Halladale* (55 cars). During the winter period she was frequently laid up but was used to cover the Folkestone–Calais workings of the passenger steamer *Cote d'Azur* while also assisting from time to time on the Dover–Boulogne car ferry link.

Any freight on offer was shipped via the Dover–Dunkirk train ferry service and so the car ferries of this early generation did not require a great deal of headroom; the *Compiegne*'s being just 3.85 metres. Nevertheless, she represented a huge technological advance, was very much a pioneer

ship and boasted a number of innovations which were quickly taken up by other operators.

She was the first cross-Channel ship to be fitted with variable-pitch propellers so that the Captain had immediate control of the ship's speed through his bridge combinators. Secondly, the ship was also fitted with a stern bridge for ease of navigating astern into Dover and Calais. For a while this idea proved very useful although they appear to have been more popular with Marine Superintendents than with Masters who preferred to remain on their bridge wings in order to have an overall view of matters when docking. A third innovation was the ship's bow-thrusters which pushed the vessel gently onto or away from the quay while fourthly, she was built of all-welded construction which allowed a degree of prefabrication and therefore speed during the building process.

The *Compiegne*'s success saw the *Chantilly* enter service for the 1966 season after which the roll on–roll off revolution snowballed and required a complete and total reappraisal in the basic design of cross-Channel vehicle ferries.

The versatile *Chartres* followed for the 1974 season, her dimensions

*On 29th September 1981, the new **Cote d'Azur** underwent trials at Folkestone and is seen off the port awaiting the departure of the **Horsa** for Boulogne. (FotoFlite)*

The **Cote d'Azur** *speeding towards the western entrance of Dover Harbour during her berthing trials on 28th September 1981. (FotoFlite)*

being limited in order to fit Dover's train ferry dock. Her near sisters BR's *Vortigern* and ALA's *Saint Eloi* eventually replaced the original trio of train ferries although the *Chartres* and *Vortigern* maintained car ferry rosters during the summer when they operated as drive-through ferries.

The 1980s would see a further development in the construction of vehicle ferries and witness the most intensive period of competition between the rival fleets of Townsend Thoresen and the Sealink partners - British Rail (Sealink UK Ltd) and SNCF Armement Naval. Each provided three ferries with twin vehicle decks, necessitating improved port infrastructure in the form of linkspans at both Dover and Calais. For Townsend Thoresen, the *Spirit of Free Enterprise, Herald of Free Enterprise* and *Pride of Free Enterprise* were built by SUAG at Bremerhaven. All arrived on time and were in service for the 1980 season. Sealink UK Ltd had their *St Anselm* and *St Christopher* built by Harland & Wolff at Belfast and both were very late in arriving. SNCF's contribution to the revitalised service was their third named *Cote d'Azur*. She too, was also late.

THE NEW SHIP

Yard number 256 was constructed at Le Havre by Ateliers et Chantiers du Havre; her keel was laid on 18th April 1980 and she was launched on 22nd December. Delivery was expected on 16th August the following year but following trials, it was not until 26th September that the ship actually arrived at Calais. In the meantime, the *Chartres* was utilised to operate the French third of Sealink's Dover–Calais link which was marketed as the

'Flagship Service' in opposition to Townsend Thoresen's 'Blue Riband Route'.

The £16 million ship boasted ten decks with passenger accommodation being spread over three of them; letters rather than numbers being originally used. Thus the boat deck was Deck H (later Deck 8), the main passenger deck was Deck G (later Deck 7) while Deck F (later Deck 6) contained galleries down both sides in which additional seating areas were placed.

Her accommodation was greatly superior to that of her British counterparts, not only from the point of view of space but also in style. Early press releases pointed to the fact that her designers had made every effort to maximise views of the sea from the ship's lounges and this was most noticeable when compared with her operating partners the *St Anselm* and *St Christopher* which both appeared claustrophobic by comparison.

At the after end of Deck H was the Bar du Soleil while midships were the Nursery, a ladies salon and two private cabins. Officers' cabins occupied the forward end of this deck. Above this on Deck I were the after bridge, the emergency generator room, the ventilation and air-conditioning control room, the radio room and the bridge while Deck J housed the base of the funnel.

The bulk of the accommodation was on Deck G with the Bar du Saint Tropez forward and the bureau de change and Information desk (Purser) immediately aft of this in the ship's main lobby. Further astern along the ship's centre line, was the Buffet Express behind which were the Boutiques (alcohol, perfume and tobacco) with seated promenades outboard while at the after end was sited the self-service restaurant and a dining room for lorry drivers. The passport office was sited between the boutiques and the restaurant.

Below on Deck F, the port side gallery housed the Salon de la Croisette (forward), which was used as a conference room and cinema, and the Salon de l'Esterel while on the starboard side was the Salon de la Baie des Anges.

Decks C, D and E were vehicle decks with Deck D being a removable mezzanine deck for private cars. Deck E housed the upper vehicle deck down the ship's centre line while on the port side were the ship's stores and cold-storage rooms with crew cabins being placed along the starboard side.

Deck B was the Engine Deck which housed the engine control room and crew cabins while Deck A was the engine room itself. Twin 18-cylinder SEMT-Pielstick 18PC2/5V diesel engines built by Alsthom Atlantic at Saint Nazaire and developing 22,500 hp, drove the ship at 20.5 knots on trials. The engines were designed to run on 180 CST heavy fuel oil at 50 degrees C, turning at a constant speed of 500 rpm. The furnishing of the ship's passenger spaces was by Chantiers A. Baudet of Saint Nazaire and based on the designs of Nantes-based M. Lionel Bureau. The company has an illustrious pedigree and also designed interiors for the liners *Normandie, France* and *Queen Mary 2* as well as for many present-day cruise ships. La Maison du Mobilier, designer-decorators from Le Havre, were responsible for fitting out the officers' quarters, the lorry-drivers' dining room and the ladies' rest room. The majority of the seats on board were of SNCF railway carriage design supplied by the Sofanor Company (764 seats of coach type Z6400 and 66 seats of Z2 railcar type) while the decorative panel in the hall on G Deck was designed and produced by M. Francois Saladin.

INTO SERVICE

With berthing trials carried out at Dover on 28th September, more were performed at both Folkestone and Boulogne on the following day.

It is unfortunate that problems over manning levels have led to a series of strikes following the introduction of a number of new French ferries and the *Cote d'Azur*'s entry into service was marred by a period of industrial unrest. The ship's maiden commercial voyage took place at 07.15 from Calais on 7th October but the planned naming ceremony had to be postponed from 27th October until her London visit on 2nd December.

On 1st December, the new *Cote d'Azur* visited the Pool of London where she berthed alongside HMS *Belfast*. There she was thrown open to the press and public while her vehicle decks were converted into large show rooms displaying a variety of French goods. An announcement was also made that her passenger certificate would be raised from 1,400 to 1,596. The occasion was an excellent public relations event and a photograph was even released showing the ship passing through Tower Bridge. Unfortunately this proved to be totally bogus as she passed through the famous portals during the hours of darkness! She eventually left London on 6th December and was back in service two days later.

The ship's darkest hour undoubtedly occurred on 5th August 1982 when on the 02.00 sailing from Dover she was involved in a collision with the *Chantilly* in which both ships received badly damaged stems. Resulting from this, the *Cote d'Azur* was sent to Dunkirk where her smashed bow visor was removed and the watertight door behind it was welded up for the rest of the season. The ship continued in service but as a stern loader which caused operational delays and problems with the freight. Her October overhaul saw the bow visor reinstalled and she re-entered service on 20th December.

*The **Cote d'Azur** fitting out at Le Havre. (Nigel Thornton collection)*

The ship's Boutiques were situated down the centre line of G Deck (Deck 7). (SeaFrance)

The Bar du Soleil was on H Deck (Deck 8), below the after bridge, and commanded excellent views across the ship's stern. (SeaFrance)

The promenade on the starboard side of G Deck; the seats were of SNCF railway carriage design.
(SeaFrance)

A 2009 view of the port side boat deck looking aft beneath the lifeboat davits as the **SeaFrance Rodin**
heads towards Dover in the distance. (John Hendy)

The **Champs Elysees** (left) and **Cote d'Azur** cross each other in Dover Harbour as the former heads
towards the Admiralty Pier to operate a train-connected service to Calais. (John Hendy)

The entry into service of the very similar *Champs Elysees* in October 1984 coincided with an attempt to reinstate the Dover–Boulogne service which had once been pre-eminent but had ceased following the joint decision of Sealink UK Ltd and SNCF Armement Naval to concentrate all traffic on Calais in competition with Townsend Thoresen. Running to Boulogne from Dover again would simply serve to weaken Sealink's overall position as all Boulogne-bound traffic sailed from Folkestone. However, between June and August 1985, the *Cote d'Azur* fitted in sailings to Boulogne between her busy Calais schedules until New Year's Day 1986 when she made the final crossing on the secondary route.

SPN AND SEAFRANCE

Sealink UK Ltd was purchased by Sea Containers during 1984 and the British ships now traded as Sealink British Ferries. There were plans to stretch the *St Anselm* and *St Christopher* to compete with Townsend Thoresen's new 'Chunnel Beaters' which were due in service in 1987 but eventually, SeaCo opted for the purchase of a pair of deep sea ro-ro vessels.

After complete rebuilds at Bremerhaven, the two ferries were renamed *Fantasia* and *Fiesta*, the latter operating for SNCF. The French ship, along with running partner *Cote d'Azur* were now registered in the ownership of SPN (Societe Propietaire des Navires) which was 49% owned by SeaCo while the *Champs Elysees* was transferred to operate the Dieppe–Newhaven service.

As a result of the setting up of the new French company, a new livery was introduced in which the *Cote d'Azur* reappeared during April 1990, although SNCF had previously adopted white hulls for their ships during the winter of 1987/88.

With the hostile takeover of Sea Containers by Stena Line in 1991, the French fleet found themselves with yet another cross-Channel partner. Whereas, their relationship with Sea Containers had frequently been strained, with the Swedish company at the helm matters became completely impossible which hastened the inevitable split in the former Sealink consortium.

As from New Year's Day 1996, the French formed SeaFrance and found themselves in competition with their former partners. Immediately, the *Cote d'Azur* was sent back to Le Havre to prepare her for the latest chapter of her Channel career as the *SeaFrance Renoir*.

MODIFICATIONS

During this most extensive refit, a total rebrand and interior modification was carried out. The most obvious change was the removal of the after stern bridge and the addition of a greenhouse-type atrium at the after end of the Bar du Soleil (now renamed La Brasserie) to house a new Cafe le Parisien on Deck 9. A waiter service restaurant was installed on the starboard side of La Brasserie which complemented the self-service restaurant on the deck below which was grandly renamed the Relais Gourmet. Copies of Renoir's most famous paintings now graced the ship which was described as 'A work of art' by the French public relations team.

Further forward on Deck G (now Deck 7), the area once occupied by the Boutiques and the Buffet Express was completely cleared out and extended, the new entrance now being sited in the ship's main lobby between Information (which was moved from the port to the starboard side) and the bureau de change. The Bar de Saint Tropez became Le Pub and was given a nautical theme with photographs of yachts lining the bulkheads.

Below on Deck F (Deck 6), the port side arcades became a Ro-Ro

*The **Cote d'Azur** heading towards Dover in the white livery that the fleet briefly adopted during the winter of 1987/88. (FotoFlite)*

The SPN livery in which the ship appeared during April 1990. (FotoFlite)

Following the formation of SeaFrance in 1996, the renamed **SeaFrance Renoir** *received major modifications to her after end. (FotoFlite)*

Passing the **SeaFrance Cezanne** *(ex* **Fiesta***) in mid-Channel. (FotoFlite)*

*The **SeaFrance Renoir** swinging in Dover Harbour as the **Pride of Calais** departs in May 2008. (John Hendy)*

*The **SeaFrance Renoir**'s main stairway with a reproduction of Renoir's famous painting, 'The Boating Party'. (John Hendy)*

Drivers' Restaurant and Kids' Corner while the starboard side was closed off. A further addition was installed on Deck 8 in the form of a Video Arcade while the ship's passenger certificate was reduced from 1,596 to its original 1,400.

It was not only the atrium which altered the ship's after end but her stern was fitted with a duck-tail sponson to improve both stability and fuel consumption. It also allowed a better fit at the wider and newer linkspans which were being built for the new generation of cross-Channel ferries. At the age of 15 and now ready to commence this new phase of her career, the new look *SeaFrance Renoir* was re-introduced into the Calais–Dover schedules in February 1996.

NEW SHIPS

With the turn of the century and a new millennium, the *SeaFrance Renoir* and the former *Champs Elysees* (now the *SeaFrance Manet*) soon became the only ships of their generation left in service across the Dover Strait. The entry into service of the excellent new *SeaFrance Rodin* in November 2001 saw the 'Renoir' withdrawn and laid up at Dunkirk thereafter reappearing in a reserve capacity and at peak periods.

April 2002 saw the *SeaFrance Renoir* unusually spot chartered by Norfolkline, operators of the Dover–Dunkirk West route. With their *Northern Merchant* and *Midnight Merchant* away on refit, the company required a back-up vessel in order to maintain schedules. With nothing suitable on offer, an agreement with SeaFrance was secured for extra working on the Calais–Dover service and the 'Renoir' was reactivated to operate it.

During 2003 the ship was brought back into service and operated a full roster but after the arrival of the *SeaFrance Berlioz* in March 2005, her career appeared to be over. However, operating with a six-ship fleet (although never all at the same time), she continued and in September 2005, the 'Renoir' replaced the newer 'Manet' on the full-time roster while the latter continued in a thrice-daily freight capacity. This may have seemed an odd move but the 'Renoir's' passenger accommodation was more extensive and she had received the benefit of that major refit during the winter of 1995/96.

In December 2007, SeaFrance announced the purchase of the

*Through the car windscreen: driving on board the **SeaFrance Renoir**'s lower vehicle deck. The upper ramp can be seen at the very top of the picture. (John Hendy)*

Following the 1996 modifications, the former Bar du Soleil, aft on Deck 8, was renamed La Brasserie. (John Hendy)

A classic view of the **SeaFrance Renoir** *as she swings off the Eastern Docks berths at Dover in March 2007. (John Hendy)*

The **SeaFrance Renoir** *shows a clean pair of heels as she leaves the West Pier at Calais astern. (John Hendy)*

'Superfast' *Jean Nicoli,* the ship that became the *SeaFrance Moliere,* and it was stated that she would replace both the *SeaFrance Renoir* and the *SeaFrance Manet.* The 'Manet' finally completed her sailings in April 2008 with the *SeaFrance Cezanne* (ex *Fiesta*) also finishing in February 2009 mainly thanks to the thumping operational losses which SeaFrance had accumulated and which had brought the company to its knees. The future SeaFrance would see a greatly reduced fleet with many redundancies. The company's failure to invest in replacement tonnage had certainly aggravated the precarious situation in which they now found themselves.

Yet still the *SeaFrance Renoir* continued in service throughout 2008 taking up the 'Manet's' freight crossings after her withdrawal and playing a vital role when brought back into full service following the fire that closed the Channel Tunnel in September. Her work continued during the early 2009 refit period and then again in May when the *SeaFrance Moliere* went off service for a further fortnight with bow-thrust and gearbox problems.

The 'Moliere's' return to traffic on Tuesday 26th May brought about the inevitable when the *SeaFrance Renoir* worked her final sailing with the 07.00 from Dover to Calais after which it was 'finished with engines' and the ship was sent to lay by in Calais.

RETROSPECT

The writer made a final crossing during the 'Renoir's' last week in service and the experience proved to be something of an eye-opener. The ship that had heralded a new beginning for her owners and the 'Flagship Service' had become something of a museum piece and an anachronism. As the final representative of her generation remaining in service on the route for which she was built, the ship was now simply too small and therefore uneconomic to operate. Ferry design had moved on apace within her remarkable 28-year career but how grateful one was for her comfortable lounges, compact interior and outside deck space from which to leisurely enjoy the Channel breezes – a fact which most present day designers sadly choose to ignore.

The *Cote d'Azur / SeaFrance Renoir* proved to be a most reliable and dependable ferry, outlasting all her contemporaries with ease and earning herself a place in the local record books for vehicle ferry longevity. Her modern yet traditional profile was a constant delight and was always so easy on the eye, combining as it did the strengths of the past with 1980's modernity. With a strong funnel sited in the 'proper' position between two slender, raked, masts and with her pleasantly rounded forward superstructure, the longest serving SNCF car ferry stood out amongst the others in the Dover Strait.

We'll not see her like again.

SNCF/ SEAFRANCE VEHICLE FERRIES – A COMPARISON

	COMPIEGNE	CHARTRES	COTE D'AZUR	SEAFRANCE RODIN
Year	1958	1974	1981	2001
Gross tons	3,467	4,590	8,479	33,796
Length (oa)	115.03m	115.40m	130.03m	185.82m
Beam (Extr)	8.35	19.23	23.02	27.70
Draft (Max)	4.03	4.19	5.00	6.50
Passengers	1,000	1,400	1,400/1,596	1,900
Cars	160	240	330	700
Lorries		22	54	120

*The **SeaFrance Renoir** in the ARNO dry dock at Dunkirk in December 2006. (John Hendy)*

Almost the end: leaving Calais on 21st May 2009. (John Hendy)

*During September 2009, the **SeaFrance Renoir** is seen laid up for sale at Dunkirk East. (John Hendy)*

*With open bridge wings and passenger access running the full length of her Boat Deck, the elegant **SeaFrance Renoir** is seen at her best. (FotoFlite)*

2 Liverpool
by Ian Collard

When I first became interested in ships in the early 1960s the Port of Liverpool and its ships were totally different to what they are today. Many of the major United Kingdom shipping operators sailed from the Port and several were based in Liverpool. The Clan Line had operated from Liverpool since the line bought two sailing ships in 1877 to provide a service from Liverpool to Bombay and by 1881 they also operated services from Glasgow and Liverpool to India and South Africa and later to East Africa, Chittagong and Buenos Aires.

Alfred Holt's Blue Funnel Line purchased a three-masted sailing ship in 1852 and the Ocean Steamship Company was formed in 1865 with the *Agamemnon* sailing from Liverpool to the Far East on 19th April 1866, calling at Penang, Singapore, Hong Kong and Shanghai. John Reeves Ellerman became the managing director of Frederick Leyland & Company in 1892 and when he became the Chairman of the company he sold various aspects of the firm but retained the Mediterranean, Portuguese, Antwerp and Montreal parts of the business. The name of the line was changed to Ellerman Line in 1901 and the following year the fleet of William S. Westcott & Laurence was added, providing the company with a service from London.

In 1839 Thomas Harrison went into partnership with George Brown who operated a shipbroking business in Liverpool. He was joined by his brother James in 1848 and when George Brown died in 1853 the company became known as Thomas & James Harrison. The Brocklebank Line was one of the oldest shipping companies in the world and was always associated with the Indian trade. Thomas and John Brocklebank opened an office in Liverpool in 1819 and ran a shipping service to Calcutta. The departure of the wooden paddle steamer *Britannia* from Liverpool to New York on 4th July 1840 marked the beginning of one of Britain's most well-known shipping companies. Samuel Cunard had arrived in Liverpool from Canada in 1839 and by 1862 their first screw-propelled mail ship, the *China* was delivered to the Cunard Line.

The Union Cold Storage & Ice Company was established in Liverpool in 1897 by Edmund and William Vesty to provide refrigerated storage for meat products and the transport of meat from Australia to the United Kingdom. When the Royal Mail Lines refused to give them preferential rates for their cargo they decided to charter vessels to bring their products to Britain and the Blue Star Line was formed in 1911. The Anchor Line name dates back to 1852 when two sailing ships were purchased for services to South America and India and the Bibby Line, founded by John Bibby owned 18 ships trading to Lisbon, the Mediterranean, South America and Bombay in 1836.

The other major shipping lines to operate services from Liverpool were the Elder Dempster Line, Canadian Pacific Steamships, Pacific Steam Navigation Company, Shaw Savill, Royal Mail Lines, Furness Withy, Booth Line, Lamport and Holt, Houlder Brothers, Prince Line, Johnson and Warren, Union Castle and Port Line. The India Steamship Company, the Danish J. Lauritzen, Lykes Bothers, Nigerian National Line, Rickmers, the Indian Scindia Steam Navigation Company, Ove Skou, NYK Line and the United States Lines all operated regular services from the Port of Liverpool.

The Mersey Docks and Harbour Board was created in 1857 following a Royal Commission which had been set up to investigate complaints by merchants who were dissatisfied as they felt that their dues paid to the Corporation were being spent on the town of Liverpool and not on the harbour or the facilities in the docks. Langton Dock, Alexandra Dock and a new graving dock at Canada Dock were constructed and Gladstone and Gladstone Graving Dock were opened on 11th July 1913. The electrification of the whole system was completed in 1925 and Clarence Dock power station also generated electricity for parts of Lancashire and Cheshire. On the Wirral side of the river, Morpeth and Alfred Docks had been built and the Great Float was completed in 1866. New entrances were built at Alfred Dock, Vittoria Dock and graving docks were constructed and Bidston Dock was completed in 1933.

A feasibility study on the extension of the dock system was completed in 1964 and this was sanctioned by the Government in 1967. However, because of various stoppages and disputes in the late 1960s many days were lost and ships were diverted to other ports. When the Port was unable to meet its debts a bill was put before Parliament in 1970 to make the Port Authority a statutory company and the following year the Board was changed to the Mersey Docks and Harbour Company which freed it from many of its responsibilities and obligations. The new Royal Seaforth Dock was opened that year and in 1973 the north docks system was closed to traffic.

The new Royal Seaforth Dock was built to provide deeper docks and longer berths supported by extensive land areas for larger ships and container services with specialized accommodation. The new dock enabled the Port of Liverpool to enter a new phase in its history and to provide modern and up-to-date facilities for larger vessels and specialised container ships. The first two container ships to use the new berths were the Ellerman Line's *Tagus* and the MacAndrews' *Cervantes* which arrived at Seaforth in the first week of May 1972. The new dock system also incorporated a Grain Terminal berth to accommodate vessels up to 75,000 tons with facilities to feed grain directly to mills on the site, a meat unloading and specialized timber berths.

For over a century the Port of Liverpool had been the most important port terminal for the amount of cargo by sea to and from Ireland. At the end of the 1960s there were more than ten coastal services operating from Liverpool to Dublin, Belfast, Larne and the other smaller Irish ports. In addition approximately 1,300,000 passengers travelled across the Irish Sea each year between Liverpool-Dublin, Liverpool-Belfast and Douglas, Isle of Man. The increase in demand for shipping cargo in unit loads enabled Coast Line's to inaugurate a new service by Link Line from Trafalgar Dock. In 1970 just over 12,000 tons of cargo passed through the port to and from the Republic of Ireland and 7,500 tons to and from Belfast.

The Isle of Man Steam Packet invested in two side-loading car ferries, *Manx Maid* and *Ben-my-Chree* in 1962 and 1966 respectively. The Belfast Steamship Company introduced the car ferries *Ulster Prince* and *Ulster Queen* in 1967 and invested in a completely new terminal at Princes Dock, Liverpool. The B+I Line was owned by Coast Lines until it was sold to the Irish Government in 1965. The car ferries *Munster*, *Leinster* and *Innisfallen* were built for the service between Liverpool and Dublin and Swansea to Cork. A passenger terminal was built at Trafalgar Dock, Liverpool and in 1980 the company operated the first fast craft service in the Irish Sea with the jetfoil *Cu-na-Mara* (Hound of the Sea), from Liverpool landing stage to Dublin. The *Cu-na-Mara* re-entered service the following year but because of mechanical problems, the increased price of fuel and decline in tourism in Ireland she was withdrawn, laid up at Arklow and sold to Japanese owners in 1985.

It was during this period that the passenger liners operating from the port began to feel the competition from the airlines and were gradually withdrawn because of dwindling passenger numbers. The Bibby Line passenger service from Birkenhead to Rangoon ceased in 1965 and Anchor Line's *Circassia* took the final passenger sailing between Glasgow and Liverpool to Bombay the following year. Elder Dempster Line's *Accra*, was sold for scrapping in 1967 after only 20 years of service; the *Apapa*, was sold the following year while the *Aureol* survived until 1972 when she took her last West African passenger sailing from Liverpool before being transferred to Southampton. The *Empress of Britain* was sold to the Greek Line in 1964, the *Empress of England* became the *Ocean Monarch* in 1970 and the *Empress of Canada* was sold to the Carnival Corporation in 1972. The *Sylvania* sailed on Cunard Line's last sailing from Liverpool to New York on 24th November 1966 and the *Carinthia* made the line's last passenger voyage from Liverpool to Montreal in 1967.

The Isle of Man Steam Packet decided to abandon its Liverpool route and the *Mona's Queen* took the last sailing from the port on 30th March 1985. B+I Lines *Connacht* and *Leinster* were introduced on their Liverpool-Dublin service between 1978 and 1981 and an experimental passenger service from Dublin to Holyhead commenced in 1982. Following the closure of the Waterloo river entrance it was announced that the Liverpool-Belfast passenger service would close and the two B+I vessels on the Dublin service were transferred to a new berth at Brocklebank Dock. The *Connacht* and the *Leinster* continued on the service until 1988 when the vessels were transferred to the Dublin to Holyhead route. However, in April that year Sealink placed the *Earl William* on the Liverpool to Dun Laoghaire service but this was closed in 1990 with the final sailing from Dun Laoghaire to Liverpool on 9th January that year. The winter service from Douglas to Liverpool was resumed by the *Lady of Mann* on 12th January 1991 after a gap of five years.

The Irish Continental Line car ferry *Saint Patrick* was transferred to the Liverpool-Belfast service in 1982 and renamed *Saint Colum 1* until the service was closed in 1990. However, in November 1991 Norse Irish Ferries started a service between the two ports using the chartered *Norse Lagan* and *Norse Mersey*. The service proved to be successful and in 1996 Norse Irish Ferries announced that they had placed an order for two passenger and freight ships which were given the names *Mersey Viking,* and *Lagan Viking*. In 1999 Norse Irish Ferries were taken over by Cenargo and operated with the *Brave Merchant* and the *Dawn Merchant* which had been introduced on the Liverpool-Dublin service by Merchant Ferries in 1998. It was expected that the *Mersey Viking* and *Lagan Viking* would be replaced on the Belfast route by two new-buildings, the *Midnight Merchant* and the *Northern Merchant* but on completion they were chartered to Norfolkline for their services out of Dover. In 2002 the Belfast and Dublin services

*The Elder Dempster Line's **Apapa** (1948/11,607 gross tons) and **Aureol** (1951/14,083 gross tons) in Brocklebank Dock, Liverpool in 1968. The **Apapa** was sold to Hong Kong owners and renamed **Taipooshan** in 1968. She survived until 1975 when was she was sold for scrapping at Kaohsiung. The **Aureol** was built in 1951 on the Clyde for the company's West Africa passenger and freight service and was named after a mountain in Sierra Leone. In 1972 she was transferred to Southampton and was laid up but in 1974 she was sold to the National Shipping Corporation of Pakistan. However, when that sale fell through she was sold for use as an accommodation ship at Jeddah and was renamed **Marianna VI** in 1975. The ship was finally broken up at Alang in 2001 and had been laid up at Eleusis, Greece since 1991.*

were transferred to the new river berth at Twelve Quays, Birkenhead and in 2005 it was announced that Norse Merchant would charter two new ships which were named *Mersey Viking* and *Lagan Viking*. The previous holders of the names were renamed *Dublin Viking* and *Liverpool Viking* and from 2005 the services were operated under the name of Norfolkline. P&O offer three sailings a day from Liverpool's Gladstone Dock to Dublin with the former Hull-based vessels *Norbay* and *Norbank* and the chartered *Celtic Star* while Seatruck offer two sailings a day on the same route.

Following the closure of the passenger liner services the port has seen several cruise liners visit. CTC Cruise Lines commenced using Liverpool as a cruise port in 1992 and the Royal Caribbean Line vessels *Sun Viking* and *Song of Norway* have visited the port. Cunard Line's *Crown Dynasty* and the company's flagship *Queen Elizabeth 2* called at Liverpool for the first time on 24th July 1990. In 1997 Direct Holidays announced that they would be operating a series of cruises from Liverpool the following year. These were operated by the *Edinburgh Castle* which was previously the Italian liner *Eugenio Costa* and would follow on the success of CTC Lines' *Southern Cross* which had been operating out of Liverpool on similar cruises. The *Edinburgh Castle* was also joined by the *Apollon* which was launched as the *Empress of Canada* and had operated out of Liverpool on Canadian Pacific Steamships Canadian services. However, mechanical problems with both ageing vessels forced the line to cancel several of the cruises. Direct Line were taken over by Airtours in 1998 who announced that the cruise programme would not operate after the 1999 season.

Liverpool was included in several cruise programmes and the *Queen Eizabeth 2* visited the port on her Round Britain cruises. However, the situation was not ideal as the cruise liners would have to anchor in the centre of the river and passengers would be taken ashore by the Mersey Ferries. The river has a reputation for its strong tide and on several occasions tugs had to be used to ensure the safety of the vessels. A cruise berth was located at Langton Dock which has been used in recent years by the ships of Fred Olsen Lines, Saga and other cruise vessels. However, as it is located inside the dock system it is unpopular with the major cruise operators who would prefer to use a river terminal. The original stage had been demolished and a smaller landing stage to accommodate the Manx and Mersey ferries had been opened in 1977.

Consequently, it was announced that a new cruise facility would be built at the Pier Head next to the ferries berth and this was opened with the visit of the *Seven Seas Voyager* in 2007. It is one of the few cruise terminals in the world that is located within walking distance of a city centre and it was visited by ten cruise liners in 2008. Negotiations are taking place with the owners of the cruise facility, Liverpool City Council, Peel Ports, Fred. Olsen and Saga regarding the use of the terminal to enable passengers to begin and end their cruise at the new terminal. The first cruise vessel to offer this service is the *Queen Mary 2* which advertised voyages to and from Southampton in October 2009. The return of the liners to the Mersey will provide a welcome boost to the local economy and maintain the strong maritime links the region has to the rest of the world.

Shaw Savill Line's **Ocean Monarch** *(1956/25,585 gross tons) in dry dock at Cammell Laird, Birkenhead in 1970. She was built as the* **Empress of England** *for the Canadian Pacific services to Quebec and Montreal. She was chartered to the Travel Savings Association in 1963 and was returned to the Liverpool-Montreal route in 1965. She was then sold to Shaw, Savill & Albion in 1970 and renamed* **Ocean Monarch** *and completed one voyage to Australia before arriving at Cammell Laird for refitting as a one-class liner. She was engaged in cruising from Sydney in 1973 but suffered from breakdowns and mechanical problems. Returning to the United Kingdom she was withdrawn in 1975 and was sold to be broken up at Kaohsiung.*

*The **Sylvania** (1957/21,989 gross tons) in Huskisson Dock, Liverpool in 1967. She was employed on Cunard Line's Canadian and New York services. She was sold to the Sitmar Line in 1968 and renamed **Fairwind**, briefly **Sitmar Fairwind**, and became the **Dawn Princess** in 1988 and then **Albatros** in 1993. She was further renamed **Genoa** in 2004 for her delivery voyage to Alang to be broken up.*

*The **Queen Elizabeth 2** in the River Mersey*

Transocean Tours' **Marco Polo** *(1965/22,080 gross tons) anchored in the River Mersey. She was originally built as the Russian liner* **Alexandr Pushkin** *and became the* **Marco Polo** *in 1991.*

A regular visitor to the Mersey was Fred. Olsens's **Black Prince** *(1966/11,209 gross tons) which is seen leaving the Langton Lock during her last year in service in 2009.*

The Isle of Man Steam Packet Company's **Manxman** *(1955/2,495 gross tons) berths at Princes Landing Stage, Liverpool.*

The five 'classic' Isle of Man vessels **Manxman** *(1955/2495 gross tons),* **Mona's Isle** *(1951/2,491 gross tons),* **Tynwald** *(1947/2,487 gross tons),* **Snaefell** *(1948/2,489 gross tons) and* **King Orry** *(1946/2,485 gross tons) usually spent most of the winter laid up at Morpeth Dock, Birkenhead.*

The Wallasey Corporation ferries **Egremont** (1952/566 gross tons) and **Leasowe** (1951/567 gross tons) at Liverpool Landing Stage preparing to sail to New Brighton and Seacombe.

B+I Line's **Leinster** (1948/4,115 gross tons) moves astern in Princes Dock. She was renamed **Leinster 1** and **Aphrodite** in 1969 and was finally broken up in 1988.

*The **SuperSeaCat Two** (1997/3,500 gross tons) in the River Mersey. She was renamed **Viking** in 2008 but replaced by the **Manannan** in May 2009 and has since been sold.*

*The **Brave Merchant** (1998/22,152 gross tons) arrives in the Mersey on a stormy December day.*

The **Liverpool Viking** passes her sister ship **Dublin Viking** off New Brighton in 2006.

P&O's **European Envoy** (1979/18,653 gross tons) sails from Gladstone Dock to Dublin. She was sold in 2004 to Stena A/B and later resold to KystLink A/S, Norway and renamed **Envoy**.

The Steam Packet's **Lady of Mann** *(1976/3,083 gross tons) passes P&O's* **Norbank** *(1993/17,464 gross tons) off Crosby.*

Saga Line's **Saga Rose** *(1965/ 24,528 gross tons) anchored off the Pier Head at Liverpool. She was built as the* **Sagafjord** *and was sold to the Cunard Line in 1983 becoming the* **Gripsholm** *in 1996. The vessel was acquired by Saga Shipping in 1997, renamed* **Saga Rose** *and is due to retire in December 2009.*

3 Cruising the Red Sea

by Richard Seville

The pilgrim trades across the Red Sea, carrying the faithful and migrant workers between Egypt, Jordan and Saudi Arabia, have often been the final home for former European ferries. However, even today in the Internet age, frustratingly little is known about these fascinating services - with the exception of a disturbingly consistent flow of reports of founderings, collisions and fires - often with devastating loss of life.

Numerous familiar names have been lost in the area, the former *Free Enterprise VI*, *Ulster Queen* and *Boccaccio* to name just three. Due to the political climate and restrictions within these countries, independent travel for the purposes of photography is ill-advised if not impossible, but a gradually increasing cruise trade to the area provides the opportunity for a glimpse into this market. Having long wished to visit the region, over Easter 2009 I finally boarded the *Thomson Spirit* in Sharm el Sheikh for a seven-night Red Sea Magic itinerary.

THOMSON CRUISES

Thomson Cruises have been offering this circuit seasonally using one of their two former Holland America Line sisters, the *Thomson Spirit* and *Thomson Celebration*, which date from 1983/84 as the *Nieuw Amsterdam* and *Noordam* respectively. Built at St Nazaire, they were the Line's first purpose-built cruise ships since the ill-fated *Prinsendam* of 1973.

After displacement from the fleet, the *Nieuw Amsterdam* was sold to United States Lines in 2000 to become their *Patriot* for year-round service to Hawaii, an operation which failed in the wake of 11th September and which saw her laid up for a significant period before sale to Louis Cruise Lines in 2003 and an immediate charter to Thomson. She was joined by her sister direct from the HAL Fleet in 2006 and the two have since alternated running the Red Sea Magic itinerary annually between October and April while spending the remainder of the year in European waters.

The schedule sees a two-day stop in Aqaba, Jordan, a day cruising up the Gulf of Suez, a day at Port Sohkna and then two final days at Safaga. The key appeal of this cruise is the opportunity to visit three key archaeological sites ... namely Petra, the Pyramids and the Valley of the Kings and the area also offers excellent opportunities for diving - whilst personally, at least two of the stops were also major ferry ports. Prices for the cruise are competitive, particularly at short notice, and given they include the five-hour flight to Egypt, a very reasonable per diem of below £100 can easily be found. Due to the time of year, and the school holidays, it was unsurprising that the *Thomson Spirit* was sailing full on our cruise, but from

*The **Thomson Spirit** during her stopover at the industrial port of Port Sohkna. The 1983 built vessel still retains an unaltered profile from her Holland America days.*

Namma Lines' **Mawaddah***, formerly Minoan Lines'* **King Minos** *of 1972, at anchor in the outer harbour at Safaga.*

check-in at Gatwick to our luggage arriving in a cabin, everything went extremely smoothly and our journey was relaxed and enjoyable. Soon, we were on deck enjoying the sunshine with drinks in hand, happily anticipating the next week at sea.

ON BOARD

Sharm el Sheikh is an uninspiring, sprawling resort, not worth investing any time in exploring. The key attraction as a departure port is the uncluttered harbour and close proximity of the charter airport, along with easy access to hotels for those staying another week on land. With limited nautical interest in the port, I spent much of the first evening getting to know the vessel, whose layout is largely original. On board, she carries a slightly careworn air, with only limited refurbishment having taken place since her HAL days, but the abundance of vestiges of both her HAL and United States Lines career only served to add to the interest personally, and overall she was most comfortable.

Her key facilities are located on Deck 5, which contains a Card Room and Browsers' Internet Library forward, followed by the Explorers' Lounge to port and cinema to starboard, with the main port side arcade then leading through her shopping street, adjacent to the Raffles Bar to the main Broadway Show Lounge. The deck is completed with the buffet style Lido Restaurant aft and a spacious terrace and pool area.

Deck 4 contains the waiter service Compass Rose Restaurant midships along with the Reception Desk, whilst Deck 6 houses the upper level of the two tier Broadway Show Lounge and aft, the High Spirits bar and nightclub. The latter deck also houses a generous wraparound promenade, whilst further sundeck space is located aft of Deck 8 as well as above the bridge high up on Deck 14. Her main facilities are completed with the

Horizon Bar forward on Deck 11 and a spacious sports area forward of the funnel. Whilst limited refurbishment has taken place, notably in the High Spirits Bar, several of the spaces are almost entirely unaltered from new, including the Compass Rose Restaurant, the Explorers' Lounge and the Horizon Bar. The Explorers' Lounge, used by Thomson as a quiet lounge and for evening classical recitals, contains a series of figureheads from HAL whilst the dark wooden panelled Horizon Bar retains displays of nautical instrumentation. With great views forward, this attractive saloon was the perfect spot for both afternoon coffee and pre-dinner drinks, with Thomson providing a pianist throughout the evening. Throughout the ship many other reminders of her past careers could be found, including a number of Dutch maps displayed as murals and traditional Hawaiian artwork in the stairwells. The majority of her cabins are also original, with only the larger suites having seen significant refurbishment. Nonetheless, although a little dated, our outside twin on Deck 2 was comfortable and spacious.

AQABA

The first morning found us creeping up the Gulf of Aqaba, which is surrounded by four different countries; Egypt, Israel, Jordan and Saudi Arabia. Aqaba itself is located in Jordan, but is just a few kilometres from both the Israeli and Saudi borders. The town itself is a dirty, ramshackle place, but is Jordan's only seaport and, for tourists, is the gateway to the spectacular Wadi-Rum desert and the cliff side city of Petra. We took a full-day excursion to the so-called Red City, a two-hour coach ride away, which was well worth doing. Descending the narrow Siq, the only entrance to the city, visitors are greeted by a tantalising glimpse of the imposing Treasury before the city opens out and you can fully explore the ruins. Aqaba is also

*The former **St Columba** seen docked at Safaga whilst awaiting an evening sailing to Saudi Arabia.*

*Still retaining her Greek livery, NEL Lines' erstwhile **Aeolos Kenteris** is shown at Safaga.*

a notable ferry port, and the ferry terminal lies 7km out of town towards the Saudi border. The main local operator is Arab Bridge Maritime, who principally serve the Egyptian port of Nuweiba across the Gulf of Aqaba, a route which saves considerable time as well as avoiding the need for traffic to transit Israel. Formed in 1985, the company boasts a glitzy headquarters in the Jordanian city and their eclectic fleet currently numbers seven vessels, of which two are high-speed craft. The latter includes the *Queen Nefertiti*, formerly the *Pegasus Two* and *Tallink Auto Express 3* whilst their conventional fleet includes the one-time Fred. Olsen vessel *Borgen* of 1975 (now the *Shehrazad*) and the former *European Navigator* of P&O Irish Sea (presently the *Black Iris*). During our stay, the *Black Iris* was observed making an evening arrival whilst a further member of the fleet, the *Pella*, formerly ANEK's *Arkadi* was lying over. Arab Bridge are reported to be the recent purchasers of the former Balearia vessel *Manual Azana*, which has been renamed *Amman*. Aqaba was also busy with cruise traffic, with the *Discovery*, the *Silver Wind* and the diminutive *Athena* observed.

The third day was spent relaxing at sea, principally reading on deck and taking advantage of the pools. Although full, finding a sun lounger was not too difficult and it was a pleasure to relax on teak-lined decks. Thomson offer a varied programme of entertainment on board, ranging from genteel pursuits such as napkin folding and shuffleboard, to a variety of quizzes and interactive games. The entertainment hosts were genuinely friendly and encouraged participation without making a nuisance of themselves, whilst in addition to the main programme, there was a series of lectures concerning the classical sites to be visited. Each evening the small dance troupe would present a different production in the Broadway Show Lounge, all of which were of an excellent standard and were very well attended.

The day's events were well laid out in the on board guide, which was refreshingly devoid of the high octane sales pitch which sadly seems to characterise many of the major lines. On board extras were also kept to a minimum with free tea and coffee available throughout the day as well as ice cream in the afternoons. The catering standards were generally very good and we tended to enjoy breakfast outside whilst in the evenings alternating between the formal dining in the Compass Rose and the more relaxed atmosphere in the Lido Restaurant, where the temperature

permitted alfresco dining throughout the cruise. Efforts were made to provide reasonable variation, with special events such as Pub Lunches in Raffles Bar, where the roast beef was some of the best I've ever tasted, particularly with the home-made horseradish sauce! Passenger demographics were broad, with good representation from all ages above 30, and the overall atmosphere on board was casual and genuinely friendly; far more so than similar products which I have experienced such as Ocean Village.

SAFAGA

At the head of the Gulf of Suez, the *Thomson Spirit* berthed at Port Sohkna and excursions headed off to Cairo. Otherwise exclusively a cargo port, Port Sohkna holds little of interest to the majority of passengers, although a token souvenir stall had been set up alongside the ship and we were surprisingly free to wander around the port complex itself. The main ferry port in this region is at *Port Twefik*, approximately 50km to the north, and although tempted by a taxi ride to investigate, previous reports of inaccessible docks and the appeal of a leisurely day on a near empty *Thomson Spirit* saw us again falling into a lazy routine on board.

For the enthusiast, the final port of call, Safaga, is undoubtedly the most promising and as we arrived off there late the following morning, an array of ferries could soon be observed in the distance. As they grew ever closer, a number of familiar silhouettes could be made out at the quayside, notably the former *St Columba* of Sealink and her one-time Irish Sea rival, the former *Superferry*, both now in the colours of Namma Lines. Formed in 2005 to operate between Egypt and Saudi Arabia, the company has the declared aim of raising standards on these services. They currently have a fleet of four conventional ferries, and in addition to the *Masarrah* (ex *St Columba*) and *Mahabbah* (ex *Superferry*), the *Mawaddah*, formerly the *King Minos* of Minoan Lines, was at anchor in the harbour, meaning only the former Tirrenia vessel *Rahmah* was absent.

The company runs overnight routes from both Port Twefik and Safaga to the Saudi ports of Dhiba and Jeddah. In addition to the Namma Lines' fleet, the two brand-new Austal-built fast craft *Riyadh* and *Cairo* were laid up - commissioned by the Saudi Government as a prestigious gift to Egypt, despite having been handed over several months earlier it appeared neither

*On board the **Masarrah** - the Irish Bar (left) is now the Reception Lounge and the one-time Show Lounge is now the Al Madinah al Munawwarh cafe.*

*Still very much the **St Columba** in external profile, and **Stena Hibernia** internally, the former Holyhead favourite is seen in her latest guise as Namma Lines' **Masarrah**.*

MASARRAH

RED SEA I
www.nel.gr

had entered service and enquiries subsequently suggested that the appropriate infrastructure was not yet complete.

Notable other ferries in the port were the monohull *Red Sea 1*, the former *Aeolos Kenteris* still in NEL Lines colours, and the Greek flagged *Nicolas A* of GA Ferries, highlighting the increasing links between a number of Greek operators and Red Sea services, which have seen a series of Greek vessels either chartered or sold to the region in recent years. Passing through the vessels at anchor, to my delight, the *Thomson Spirit* berthed alongside the main ferry quays, just ahead of the *Mahabbah* providing a grandstand view of the scene and excellent photographic opportunities.

The main reason for the two-day call in Safaga are the impressive sites at Luxor and the ship duly emptied as passengers headed out on coaches in convoy. Interestingly, one of the more popular excursions sold on board was a diving trip to the wreck of the *Salem Express*, which is none other than the former *Nuits St George* used to inaugurate services between Ramsgate and Dunkirk in 1981 and later lost at sea following a fire in 1991.

We, however, had elected to spend the first afternoon on board and after lunch I took a leisurely wander along the quayside for a closer look at the ferries. The port at Safaga is a shabby, dusty place with a motley group of ramshackle buildings, mostly abandoned, and a large collection of stray dogs. All tickets are sold through agencies in the town itself, a few kilometres walk away. Both the *Masarrah* and *Mahabbah* were lying over pending evening departures but there was a steady flow of crew activity on the vehicle decks and, after a brief walk around in the company of a friendly puppy, I decided to chance my luck in asking for a visit on board. The Egyptian crew were extremely friendly and having managed to break the language barrier, to my delight my request was accepted. I was shown up to the accommodation and offered drinks, after which I was led on a top to bottom tour of the ship. The *Masarrah* still essentially remains the *Stena Hibernia*, and still to this date relatively few changes have taken place since her sale by Stena Line, with even the Stena-era fixtures and fittings remaining in the majority of areas.

The key changes include the removal and blocking off of the former Information Desk, which has been replaced by the adoption of the former Irish Bar as a Reception Lounge and the conversion of much of the former duty-free shop into a seating lounge, although a small walk round shop remains at the stern. These changes make perfect sense, as most passengers board through the aft stairwells and the duty-free shop has been largely redundant since her sale from UK waters - indeed, it is surprising that her Greek owners never made such alterations.

More minor changes included the fitting of further reclining seats into the majority of the Pantry, the closure of the Hibernia Restaurant and the creation of a new restaurant in the one-time pizzeria in addition to the installation of new theatre-style seating in the former show lounge. Namma Lines had gone to significant effort to rename all of the facilities with locally appropriate names and had also removed much of the former Stena Line branding which had survived throughout her Aegean service. As examples of the new names, the former Pantry is now the Jeddah self-service, the one-time duty-free is now the Abha Lounge and the former show lounge is the Al Madinah al Munawwrah cafe. To reinforce her new identity, many photos and pictures of Mecca decorate her bulkheads - and the vessel will clearly be at her busiest during the time of the Hajj.

Overall, although certainly well worn throughout, she was in a surprisingly clean and tidy condition given the previous reputation of Red Sea services and her crew were all interested in the information I had about her previous careers. All were happy to spend time chatting and in today's global political climate, it was a refreshing and eye-opening experience to receive such a warm welcome.

DEPARTURES

After returning to the *Thomson Spirit* for tea and cakes from the tempting afternoon buffet, I relaxed on deck astern with a grandstand view of the *Mahabbah* just metres away. Later that evening, in the same position, we observed as coaches shuttled conservatively dressed passengers to the

*The future of Red Sea services - but not just yet. The brand-new Austal built **Riyadh** is seen laid up at Safaga, awaiting entry into service.*

*Sun loungers line the aft Lido deck of the **Thomson Spirit**, with the former **Superferry** showing just how close the 'Spirit' berthed to the ferry port in Safaga.*

vessels for their pending departures. It was quite surprising the following morning therefore to see that whilst both ships had left their berths, they had only progressed to anchor in the outer harbour. It remains a mystery to me as to why they did not sail directly for their destinations but in late afternoon the *Masarrah* began emitting black smoke from her funnel and slowly headed out to sea.

Other regular callers at Safaga include the *Jaama II*, formerly the *Alandia* of Eckerolinjen and the second of the Papenburger series to serve in the region (the first, the former *Viking 1*, sank at Port Twefik in 2000) and the *Santa Catherine 3* of the much reduced fleet of El Salam Maritime - originally the *St Edmund* of Sealink. Perhaps the most astonishing survivor, which I was disappointed not to see, is the freighter *Al Zaher II*, originally SNCF's diminutive *Capitaine Le Goff* of the Dieppe to Newhaven route, which has quietly run here for nearly three decades.

The *Thomson Spirit* departed Safaga in the late evening for her final leg of the cruise, the short return crossing to Sharm el Sheikh. As we sat down to dinner in the Compass Rose Restaurant with a large, diverse group of friends we had made on board, it was with genuine sadness that I anticipated returning home. The cruise itself had exceeded all expectations; a comfortable, spacious ship with a variety of interesting reminders of her past careers; a very friendly on-board atmosphere; strong standards in catering and entertainment; excellent weather and three great destination ports ... particularly from a ferry enthusiast's point of view.

Our final morning saw all the facilities of the ship open and available to passengers until called for their transfer to the airport, enabling us to make the most of the sunshine.

Thomson Cruises come highly recommended.

*The **Mahabbah** loading for her midnight departure to Jeddah, seen from the **Thomson Spirit**.*

Photo Feature - Small Ferry Scene
by Andrew Cooke

The small ferry plays a vital part in day-to-day life around the UK with a plethora of types and styles to be found ranging from humble rowing boats to state of the art fast catamarans. Their operating environments are equally varied whilst their vital role is frequently highlighted by the media furore whenever a service comes under threat. The following gallery of photos depicts a small cross-section of what the small ferry scene has to offer.

In 1966 the Portsea-Gosport passenger ferry service across Portsmouth Harbour was revolutionised when the Thornycroft (Woolston) built sisterships **Gosport Queen** *and* **Portsmouth Queen** *were introduced. The 159 gross ton, 30.5 metre long and 250-passenger capacity vessels continue in frontline service alongside the 2001 and 2005-built* **Spirit of Gosport** *and* **Spirit of Portsmouth**. *The* **Gosport Queen** *is pictured heading for Gosport with the Semaphore Tower behind her.*

Having evolved from a 'tug and float' format to a self-propelled ferry service, the picturesque Bodinnick Ferry crosses the River Fowey from Bodinnick to Fowey in Cornwall. Operated by C. Toms & Son Ltd, the cross-river link provides a car and passenger ferry service using the **Jenack** *(shown here at Fowey) and the* **Gellan** *built in 2000 and 2003 respectively.*

Operating from Poole Quay and Sandbanks to Brownsea Island in Poole Harbour, the 1999 built, 118-gross ton, 185-passenger **Maid of Poole** *works alongside sister vessel* **Maid of the Harbour** *and two fleet mates. The unmistakable yellow boats of BIF have provided a service from Poole for over a century.*

The first regular floating bridge was conceived in 1829 and on 7th June 2009 the 48-year old diesel-electric powered, paddle driven and cable guided car and passenger ferry **Philip** *was retired in favour of a 32 car/250 passenger cable driven vessel. The 42.7- metre long, 136 passenger and 18 car capacity* **Philip** *was unique in the British Isles and built in Dartmouth in 1960.*

Until April 2007, the 73-year-old **Kenilworth** *served the Gourock-Kilcreggan-Helensburgh ferry link across the Clyde. Replaced by the* **Seabus** *she continued by offering educational cruises. Built in 1936 as the* **Hotspur II** *for the Southampton-Hythe ferry service, she was acquired by Clyde Marine Services in 1978 and renamed the* **Kenilworth** *after the novel by Sir Walter Scott. In May 2009 she began a new career on the Moray Firth for Dolphin Cruises as the* **Kelly H**.

Devon's River Dart offers a variety of ferry types including this tug and float combination operating between Kingswear and Bayard's Cove, Dartmouth. The service has existed since circa 1365 and today employs the 1989 and 1994-built floats **Tom Casey** *and* **Tom Avis** *propelled by two of three tugs, namely the* **Hauley IV/V/VI** *dating from 1965 onwards. The* **Hauley VI** *and* **Tom Avis** *are pictured arriving at Dartmouth. South Hams District Council runs the service.*

Such is the variety to be found on the River Dart that the Dittisham to Greenway ferry is also featured here. The **Dittisham Belle** *is a traditional clinker-built passenger launch and was formerly used between Looe and Looe Island as the* **Sara**. *She began life in 1982 and can carry 12 passengers.*

Once voted one of the top ten ferry crossings in the world by the 'Independent on Sunday', the King Harry Floating Bridge was first established across the River Fal in 1888. The chain ferry connects St. Mawes and the Roseland Peninsula with Feock, Truro and Falmouth. The present 2006-built chain ferry accommodates 34 cars.

The historic pedestrian and light railway pier at Hythe opened in 1881 with a passenger ferry serving Southampton across the River Test. Today two quite different vessels maintain the service. The vessel depicted is the 1946-built, 50 gross ton, 125-passenger **Hotspur IV**. *She was built by the Rowhedge Ironworks Company as were the* **Hotspur II** (**Kenilworth**) *and* **Hotspur III**. *The other vessel is the 1992-built, 162-passenger* **Great Expectations**.

The Isle of Sark Shipping Company operates two passenger vessels from St Peter Port, Guernsey, to La Maseline Jetty on the Isle of Sark. The 118-gross ton **Bon Marin de Serk** *has plied this route since new in 1983 and carries up to 131 passengers. The company also employs the 1985-built,* **Sark Venture***.*

A wonderfully rural passenger service operates from Keyhaven near Milford-on-Sea to Hurst Spit on Hampshire's Solent coastline. The tranquility of the ferry passage and shingle spit make any visit a pleasure. The seasonal operation also includes sorties to the Needles and Yarmouth, Isle of Wight. Pictured at Hurst Spit are the **Solent Rose** *(which began life as a ferry in Guernsey), the* **Haven Rose** *(since withdrawn) and the* **Catherine Rose***.*

The seasonal passenger ferry linking Starcross and Exmouth across the estuary of the River Exe in Devon is one of the longest running in the south west. With a history dating back to AD 705 the present fleet includes the twin screw diesel-powered **Orcombe**, which was built for the route in 1954.

Celebrating their 10th anniversary in 2009, Thames Clippers provides the premier commuter and leisure operation on the River Thames. Services run as far west as Waterloo and Millbank Piers and as far east as Woolwich Arsenal. A fleet of 12 catamarans now serve the company and all have names with a meteorological resonance. Pictured is the **Sun Clipper**, a 32-metre, 138-seater and 25-knot **River Runner** 150 craft built by NQEA in 2001 and bound for Greenwich.

*What better example of a small ferry than the jolly **Torquay Belle**? Built in Guernsey during 1966 as the **Typhoon** by C.P. Wilson, her unusual hull form was created after a study into how gulls float on water. Carrying up to 73 passengers and crew she plies between Torquay and Brixham for Greenway Ferry.*

*The Trident Charter Company is based in Guernsey, Channel Islands and operates the ferry service between St Peter Port and the picturesque island of Herm. The primary vessel is the 250-passenger **Herm Trident V**, a steel hulled, twin Iveco diesel-powered catamaran. Meanwhile the **Herm Trident VI**, a 1991-built sister to the **Herm Trident V**, was constructed at Gravesend shipyard in 1991. During the peak season the **Trident VI** is also chartered to the Isle of Sark Shipping Co. Both are depicted in St Peter Port Harbour embarking passengers for Herm.*

A formal ferry service has linked Torpoint (Cornwall) and Plymouth (Devon) across the River Tamar since 1791. The first floating bridge came along in 1831 and in December 2004 the first of the new generation of chain ferries, the **Plym II**, was delivered followed by the **Tamar II** and **Lynher II** in 2005/2006. The 73-metre long vessels doubled capacity on the service, carry 73 cars each and are powered by three Volvo Penta D12 engines.

At the tip of northern Scotland can be found a passenger ferry service operating across the Pentland Firth to Burwick on Orkney. The 1986-built, 186-gross ton **Pentland Venture** offers a seasonal service as well as wildlife cruises and day excursions. The custom built vessel was constructed using a hull form utilised by fishing trawlers for the best sea keeping performance.

The IoSSCo. was formed in 1919 and in 1977 took delivery of the current passenger vessel, the **Scillonian III**. Built by A&P Appledore the 1,346 gross ton, 600-passenger ship was named by HRH Prince Charles ahead of her maiden voyage on 19th May 1977. She plies between Penzance and St Mary's on the seasonal ferry service conveying all types of cargo in her hold.

The **Corran** is operated by the Highland Council between Nether Lochaber and Ardgour on Loch Linnhe in the Scottish Highlands. The ferry is located 9 miles from Fort William and forms the gateway to the Ardnamurchan peninsula. Built in 2001 by George Prior Engineering (Yorkshire) Ltd, the vessel can accommodate 150 passengers and 30 cars.

5 Holyhead Routes to Dublin Bay

by Justin Merrigan

Against a backdrop of sharp falls of up to 15% in freight traffic across its fleet, the news from Stena Line of signs of recovery on the Holyhead-Dublin route comes as little surprise. The company's Holyhead operation has always been something of a jewel in the crown, a benchmark by which other routes could be compared, even in the pre-Stena days of Sea Containers and before that, British Rail, ownership.

THE RACE FOR THE MAIL

The key factor in the development of Holyhead was the lucrative contract to carry the mail. In January 1839, the City of Dublin Steam Packet Company (CDSP) was awarded the contract to provide a night mail service from Holyhead's Admiralty Pier to Kingstown (later Dun Laoghaire), while the Admiralty was contracted to operate a day service.

The coming of the railways would greatly improve communications and on 1st August 1848 the Admiralty packets were placed on the train, the 'Irish Mail' at London Euston at 20.45, reaching Holyhead after transfer to road at Bangor at 06.45. The final section of the line, across the Menai Strait to Holyhead, opened two years later.

From 1st January 1850 the CDSP secured the contract to run both the day and the night mail service, much to the chagrin of the Chester & Holyhead Railway who had themselves ordered new steamers in the expectation that they would win the contract and place the mails in the care of the railways for the entire journey from London to Dublin. The rivalry and bitterness this caused was deep - the railway believing the contract to be rightfully theirs having invested heavily in ships and infrastructure.

This left the ships of the C&HR carrying passengers to Kingstown and also cargo and cattle to North Wall in Dublin, but without the reward of the mail contract. The company was taken over by the London & North Western Railway (LNWR) on 1st January 1859 and two years later gave up the Kingstown service, concentrating on its sailings to Dublin's North Wall, where it already operated a cargo service and had built a substantial station complete with a hotel.

Extensive new facilities in Holyhead's inner harbour were opened by the Prince of Wales in 1880. The new harbour was shaped like a 'V' with arrival and departure railway lines on either side and with transfer from train to ship being made under cover. The LNWR also opened a large hotel, ensuring close co-ordination between their trains, ships and hotel. It was against this backdrop that the railway company again expected to win the mail contract for the sea portion of the journey when it came up for renewal. And they did, three years later, but only to have it taken away again and returned to the City of Dublin Steam Packet following disruption in the House of Commons led by Irish MPs!

Meanwhile, on the Irish side, a battle of wills was raging between the Dublin Port & Docks Board and the LNWR over dues and dredging. Things eventually came to a head in 1908 when the Board raised the port dues on the LNWR's ships and the railway took this as an excuse to abandon passenger services to the North Wall and return to Kingstown. But even that was not without trouble and the CDSP protested the return of the prodigal operator to Kingstown by blockading the Carlisle Pier berths with their ships!

During World War I, the CDSP lost two steamers, the worst of which was the *Leinster* just North East of the Kish Light. Unable to recover from the losses, the company's fleet was eventually taken over by the British & Irish Steam Packet Company and the City of Dublin Steam Packet passed into the annals of history in 1924.

Meanwhile, the LNWR, anticipating their rival's problems and, with the mail contract once again going to tender, ordered four new steamers for their service; two in operation, one on standby and one for relief duties. Finally, on 28th November 1920 the Irish Mail was carried from Holyhead to Kingstown on a railway steamer, the *Anglia*, the first of the new ships.

On 1st January 1923 the LNWR became part of the London Midland and Scottish Railway. Rationalisation was the order of the day and by 1925 the *Anglia* was surplus to requirements. While passenger services to Kingstown, which had reverted to its Irish name of Dun Laoghaire in 1921, were scaled back, the railway's cargo service to Dublin also suffered through the effect of new customs requirements into Ireland.

NATIONALISATION

On the nationalisation of the railways in 1948, Holyhead's services to Dun Laoghaire and Dublin passed to British Railways, London Midland Region, under the umbrella of the British Transport Commission (BTC). Shortly afterwards, the introduction of the motorships *Hibernia* and *Cambria* finally completed an earlier plan to replace the 1920-built ships of the same names with two turbine steamers from the Clyde yard of Fairfield Shipbuilding & Engineering Co. Ltd., an order subsequently cancelled due to the onset of war. BR turned to Harland & Wolff Ltd at Belfast for the two new ships and the first of these, the *Hibernia*, arrived in Holyhead for the first time on 5th April 1949. The *Hibernia* commenced service on 14th April while the *Cambria* arrived in her home-port from Harland & Wolff's Belfast yard on 5th May.

The Shipping and International Services Department was established at the BTC in January 1957 and during the 1960s British Railways underwent a radical reorganisation, including the abolition of the BTC. The new British Railways Board (BRB) came into being on 1st January 1963 and as part of its new image, British Railways was rebranded as British Rail complete with a new corporate image and the iconic double arrow logo in late 1964.

Meanwhile, the Dublin cargo services received a boost in 1960 in the form of the *Slieve Donard*. Essentially she was a cattle boat; however, she was uniquely equipped with a vehicle deck for 100 cars and was capable of carrying up to 63 containers.

*The LNWR's **Scotia** of 1902 remained in service until replaced by a new ship of the same name in 1920. (John Hendy collection)*

*The **Holyhead Ferry 1**; such an unimaginative name for an important ship. (John Hendy collection)*

*An historic moment on 8th July 1965 as the **Normannia** berths at Dun Laoghaire for the first time. (Justin Merrigan collection)*

*The **Cambria** on No. 8, the departure berth, at Holyhead awaiting her sailing to Dun Laoghaire. (John Hendy collection)*

DRIVE ON-DRIVE OFF

The Holyhead-Dun Laoghaire route entered the car ferry age with the 1963 order for a new ship from Hawthorn Leslie (Shipbuilders) Ltd. Built at a cost of £1.6 million she was saddled with the uninspired name of *Holyhead Ferry 1* when launched on 17th February 1965. To facilitate the new ship extensive engineering works were carried out on both sides of the Irish Sea. At Holyhead the Admiralty Pier berth was modified and provided with a linkspan but at Dun Laoghaire things were not so straightforward and a temporary berth on the East Pier had to be constructed while plans for a more permanent solution were discussed.

Holyhead's new car ferry could accommodate 153 averaged size cars on her vehicle deck which was equipped with a turntable forward and aft to assist with positioning cars ready for disembarkation. A small mezzanine deck forward was accessed by hydraulically operated ramps port and starboard. Two hatches were also fitted fore and aft, primarily for loading mail into the ship but also to allow cars to be lifted out should the stern door fail. Passenger capacity was 1,000 and 64 berths were available in a variety of cabins.

The new service opened for business on 9th July 1965, not with the *Holyhead Ferry 1*, which was late from her builders, but the recently converted *Normannia* from the Dover–Boulogne run; the *Holyhead Ferry 1* finally took over on 19th July. During the height of the summer season one round trip was offered daily, departing Holyhead at 10.45 and Dun Laoghaire at 15.30. At weekends an additional round trip was offered, leaving the Welsh port at 20.15 and from Dun Laoghaire at 06.00.

The whole operation was a most civilised affair. Cabins and berths for the 06.00 sailing from Dun Laoghaire were available for occupation overnight. Passengers holding cabin and berth reservations for this sailing could report with their vehicles ready for loading between 23.30 and 23.59 the previous night. The service was a rampant success but even so it was still seasonally operated and on 17th October the route reverted to mail ship operation until the summer of 1966. Apart from the gradual extension of her Holyhead season, this routine pretty much continued for the rest of the 1960s and during the winter of 1968/69 she found herself sailing on the mail service departing Holyhead on the time-honoured 03.15 sailing on Mondays, Wednesdays and Fridays.

In 1969 Dun Laoghaire's new IR£850,000 St Michael's Wharf car ferry terminal was opened by the *Holyhead Ferry 1* on 14th March. Capable of handling 650 cars a day the new 175-metre long pier offered linkspans on both sides of the terminal. While this meant that two vessels could berth simultaneously, the principal purpose was to permit a ship to lie on the more sheltered side of the pier. The controversial temporary terminal on Dun Laoghaire's East Pier was closed that year and in four years of operation 95,000 cars had been landed at the site.

Meanwhile, the traditional cargo services to Dublin were undergoing the greatest single change since services began. Containerisation was the

*The **Holyhead Ferry 1** meets an Irish Sea gale. (Capt. Walter Lloyd Williams)*

*The **Cambria** on Dun Laoghaire's departure berth in 1969. (Capt. Walter Lloyd Williams)*

Sealink's container twins, the **Rhodri Mawr** and the **Brian Boroime** at Holyhead in 1984. (Capt. Walter Lloyd Williams)

The **Duke of Lancaster** sits on the former arrival, No. 7, berth at Holyhead while she awaits the departure of an engine troubled **St Columba** from the opposite No. 8 berth. (Ian Scott Taylor)

order of the day and works were put in place for new lift on–lift off terminals on both sides of the Irish Sea.

When the new *Rhodri Mawr* and *Brian Boroime* of 1970 entered service on routes from Holyhead to Dublin and Belfast traffic volumes grew rapidly, reaching their highest-ever annual total of 73,000 containers in 1973.

In 1973 the *Holyhead Ferry 1* had her first spell of English Channel service after which she relieved Fishguard's *Caledonian Princess* for annual overhaul. By now the 'Ferry 1' found herself based at Dover with that port's *Dover* being based at Holyhead! The reason was the latter's greater car capacity over her half-sister.

In March 1975 a £16 million order was placed with Aalborg Vaerft A/S of Aalborg, Denmark for a new Holyhead ship to replace the *Cambria* and the *Hibernia*, as well as the *Holyhead Ferry 1*. The end of the mail service came in 1975 and it fell to the *Cambria* to take the last such sailing from Dun Laoghaire on Sunday 7th September. The following day, she stood down and the *Holyhead Ferry 1* launched the new year-round multi-purpose operation. Under the command of Capt. Ivor Griffiths the *Cambria* slipped out of Holyhead for the final time at 23.00 on 28th October 1975. She arrived at Barrow at 09.00 the following morning and remained there until sold to Orri Navigation of Saudi Arabia in January 1976. Renamed *Al Taif* she sank while at anchor in Suez Roads in January 1981.

The *Hibernia* remained on the Holyhead link until Sunday 3rd October 1976 when she arrived at Holyhead with her final sailing from Dun Laoghaire. After sale to Agapitos Brothers of Greece she was renamed *Express Apollon*. On 18th December 1980 the old ship was observed at Bombay and four weeks later she was at Darukhana in India where Solid Steel Traders began demolition. As for the *Holyhead Ferry 1*, as an official Dover ship she was sent in 1976 to Swan Hunter on the Tyne for conversion to drive through operation from which she emerged renamed *Earl Leofric*.

Taking up commercial service on Monday 2nd May 1977 the new *St Columba* was an overnight success on the route. With a capacity for 2,400 passengers, 335 cars or 36 artics (or a mixture of the two) nothing quite like the ship had ever been seen before on the Irish Sea. Little wonder that after just one year in operation she had carried her one-millionth passenger. She was a much needed breath of fresh air to the service which, since the withdrawal of the *Hibernia* and the *Cambria* was operated by a variety of stop-gap steam turbine car ferries, including the *Duke of Lancaster*, the *Duke of Rothesay*, the *Duke of Argyll*, the *Caledonian Princess*, the *Avalon* and the *Dover*.

British Rail ownership of shipping services continued through the 1970s. On 1st January 1979 the Shipping and International Services Division ceased to exist and its function, assets and staff were transferred to Sealink UK Ltd., a new company wholly owned by the BRB. The brand Sealink had been used for British Rail's marine services, along with the shipping services of the continental railways organisations since January 1970.

Each summer a second ship was deployed at Holyhead to augment the *St Columba*'s sailings to Dun Laoghaire. Such notable ships as the *Duke of Lancaster*, *Avalon* and *Lord Warden* all partnered the crack ship until in 1981 a newcomer arrived in the camp fresh from Harland & Wolff - the *St David*.

PRIVATE OWNERSHIP AGAIN

Sealink UK Ltd was privatised in July 1984. In what was described as the 'Sale of the Century' the company, comprising 37 ships, 10 harbours and 24 routes, was sold to US-based Sea Containers for the incredible sum of just £66 million. Major, and much needed, investment was promised by company president Mr. James B. Sherwood and for Holyhead larger ferries were promised. In the meantime, in February 1985, the new Sealink British Ferries entered into an agreement with rivals B+I Line to rationalise sailings on the Irish Sea.

The agreement provided for co-operation between the two companies and the elimination of sailing duplication on the Holyhead and Fishguard routes to Ireland. Outwardly, this brought to an end the tradition of a second summer ship for Sealink at Holyhead - the extra sailings being covered by B+I.

Early morning arrival at Dun Laoghaire for the **Stena Cambria**. *(Miles Cowsill)*

The **Seafreight Highway** berthing at Holyhead's Admiralty Pier in 1988. (Justin Merrigan)

A newly renamed **St Cybi** (ex-**Stena Sailer**) throbs her way alongside St Michael's Pier in Dun Laoghaire. (Justin Merrigan)

With the **Stena Hibernia** outward for Dun Laoghaire, B&I's tired looking **Leinster** is passed alongside the Admiralty Pier by the inward **Stena Cambria**. (Justin Merrigan)

It was never an easy relationship and when in April 1987 Sealink introduced the freight ship *Stena Sailer* to supplement sailings of the *St Columba*, B+I cried foul and by the end of the year the partnership was at an end. It was business as usual and competition returned to Holyhead, a second seasonal passenger ship in the form of the *Horsa* being reintroduced in 1990.

By this time the steady growth in ro-ro traffic on the Irish Sea had influenced the lift on–lift off container volumes and by the early 1980s the Belfast route was being particularly affected. The end finally came in 1989 when the *Rhodri Mawr* made the last Holyhead-Dublin-Belfast container sailings on 21st December. Some 1,250,000 containers had been carried since the service began in 1971 and between them the *Rhodri Mawr* and the *Brian Boroime* had made over 18,000 crossings of the Irish Sea.

Following Sealink's acquisition by Stena Line in 1990 a massive fleet-wide investment programme was announced. This provided for significant extra capacity on the Irish Sea routes and included the introduction in June 1991 of a year-round second ferry – the *Stena Cambria*, formerly the Dover ferry *St Anselm*.

As part of the investment programme, the *St Columba* underwent an £8 million refit, designed to transform her into a floating leisure centre in with Stena's 'Travel Service Concept' which held that given top class ships, a wide range of facilities, quality entertainment and good value prices, then people would be encouraged to travel all year round, simply for the fun of the on board experience. The *St Columba* was the first ship in the rebranded Sealink Stena Line fleet to be so treated and returned to service with a new name and a very new look. As the *Stena Hibernia* she provided a huge range of facilities including an a la carte restaurant and self-service restaurant, a Pizza Factory, a Show Bar with resident band, an Irish Bar with traditional Irish music, Business Club and Conference Centre, Casino, Children's Play Area and enlarged Duty Free and Gift shops. While the adoption of the name 'Hibernia' evoked a venerable past on the Holyhead route the refit did not always meet with total approval from the travelling public. The renaming was an attempt to honour a long tradition going back almost a century and a half when the first *Hibernia* arrived at Holyhead.

HIGH SPEED - A NEW CONCEPT AFLOAT

In 1993 a further rebranded Stena Sealink Line announced that the Holyhead route would be the first in the fleet to receive a revolutionary new gas-turbine-powered high-speed craft, the High Speed Sea-Service or HSS. Pending delivery of the new vessel the company started fast craft operations with the Incat-built 74-metre *Stena Sea Lynx* from June of that year. With capacity for 425 passengers and 88 cars the *Stena Sea Lynx* reduced the three hours and 30 minutes crossing time to just one hour and 50 minutes. During her first six months in service to Dun Laoghaire the craft helped to grow the total market by over 200,000 passengers and 40,000 cars. Her immediate success led to the charter of the larger *Stena Sea Lynx II* and on 26th June 1994 the *Stena Sea Lynx* moved to the Fishguard-Rosslare service.

Delays during the construction of the HSS meant the inauguration of the new craft in time for the 1995 season failed to materialise and it was not until 10th April 1996 that the *Stena Explorer*, entered service when she sailed from the Irish port at 06.53. Her first day in service was greeted by perfect weather and some very busy crossings. Her second sailing from Dun Laoghaire saw 1,109 passengers and 223 cars loaded in little over ten minutes.

The arrival of the HSS concept on the Holyhead-Dun Laoghaire service

*New liveries at Holyhead. The **Vortigern** has received her new colours in the port's dry dock as the **St Columba** arrives from Dun Laoghaire. (John Hendy collection)*

*An unusual sight at Holyhead with the former Bateau de Luxe vessel **Earl William**. The former Channel Islands vessel had to be brought in to support the Holyhead operations in 1991, when the **Stena Cambria** had to be withdrawn from service. (Miles Cowsill)*

*The evening sun catches the **Stena Hibernia** at Dun Laoghaire. The vessel remains in service today in the Red Sea and has changed very little from her days on the Irish Sea. (see page 28). (Miles Cowsill)*

*The **Stena Challenger** arrives at Holyhead on her morning sailing from Dublin. (Miles Cowsill)*

The chartered Italian-flag **Stena Forwarder** *brought a significant increase in capacity to the Dublin operation. (Miles Cowsill)*

In 2006 a second ship for the Dublin run came in the form of the **Stena Seatrader***. (Gordon Hislip)*

The **Stena Sea Lynx II**, maintaining high speed services to Dun Laoghaire prior to the arrival of the HSS **Stena Explorer**.(Miles Cowsill)

numbered the *Stena Hibernia*'s remaining days on the Irish Sea. Renamed *Stena Adventurer* in January 1996 following the dropping of the Sealink brand and all references to previous Sealink ownership, the ship was earmarked for a transfer to Dover where her high passenger capacity would have been welcomed. In the event, the *Stena Adventurer* remained at Holyhead beyond the entry into service of the *Stena Explorer*.

While the spotlight was trained on the HSS service, another newcomer had been working away, out of the limelight, since November 1995. The *Stena Traveller* was also a key element in the company's quest to revamp travel on the Holyhead routes. This ship had replaced the *Stena Cambria* but running to Dublin Port instead of Dun Laoghaire, marking a resumption of the former British company's sailings to Dublin since the closure of the container service in 1989. This gave hauliers their own dedicated freight ship, a move welcomed by some Dun Laoghaire residents who were concerned about the increase in ro-ro traffic through their town.

Having played support to the *Stena Explorer* during the summer season, the end for the conventional ferry service to Dun Laoghaire finally came on 30th September 1996. Having completed her final sailing the *Stena Adventurer* was laid up at Dun Laoghaire and for one month the former flagship of the Sealink fleet remained on standby in the event of technical

The **Stena Traveller** brought Sealink's successor back to Dublin in 2005. (Justin Merrigan)

problems on the HSS. After this period of inactivity the ship was moved from Dun Laoghaire to Belfast for lay-up pending sale.

Before her move northwards, she was permitted one final visit to her home port, operating one round trip to clear a backlog of traffic on 29th October. The following evening the *Stena Adventurer* slipped out of Dun Laoghaire under the command of Capt. Jim Wilcox. As she left the harbour Stena Line's port vehicles lined the quay sounding their horns, a salute normally reserved for retiring Masters. In response, the *Stena Adventurer*'s whistle echoed around Dun Laoghaire as she completed her final swing before heading into Dublin Bay. Eight hours later she arrived at Belfast, Finished with Engines being rung off at 02.40 on 31st October.

On 5th April 1997, the 20th anniversary of *St Columba*'s departure from Aalborg on her delivery voyage to Holyhead, news broke of a possible sale to Agapitos Express Ferries of Greece. On 9th May, renamed *Express Aphrodite*, the ship left Belfast and the Irish Sea for the last time.

EXPANSION AT DUBLIN

The arrival of the *Stena Challenger* on the Dublin freight service in September 1996 opened the fledgling route to passengers thanks to her ability to accommodate up to 500. This ability proved its worth during the winter months when adverse weather affected HSS sailings on the Dun Laoghaire run. The *Stena Challenger* remained at Holyhead until her sale to Canadian operators in April 2001.

Replacing the *Stena Challenger* was the chartered Italian-flag *Stena Forwarder*. This ship was another boost for the service which started in 1995 as a freight only operation. With accommodation for 1,000 passengers, 500 more than her predecessor, the *Stena Forwarder* also increased freight capacity by some 60%. With the arrival of the new *Stena Adventurer* in sight, the 'Fowarder' was sold by her owners for service in Mexico. Her final sailing from Dublin was on 13th April 2003, by which time she had already been renamed *California Star*.

The arrival of Stena Line's new *Stena Adventurer* into service on the Dublin crossing during July 2003 significantly improved the company's position on the Irish Sea. Built by South Korean shipbuilder Hyundai Heavy Industries at a cost of £60 million the new ship's arrival increased passenger capacity on the Dublin route by 50% and the freight capacity by 70%.

In September 2006 Stena Line redeployed a ferry from its North Sea

*The **Stena Adventurer** overnight brought new and increased capacity to the Holyhead-Dublin service. The Korean-built vessel is seen here arriving during her first week in service on the route. (Miles Cowsill)*

*The **Stena Nordica** (ex **European Ambassador**) swings off the berth at Dublin in June 2009. (Gordon Hislip)*

fleet, the *Stena Seatrader*, to join the *Stena Adventurer* on the Dublin run. The new service completed one round trip per day increasing capacity on the corridor significantly. The addition of the *Stena Seatrader* came on the back of a successful year for Stena Line which saw total freight volumes grow by 8% during 2005. The company's five Irish Sea routes were particularly successful enjoying growth of 16%, with the biggest increase taking place on the Holyhead routes where the number of freight vehicles jumped to 173,000 units.

In July 2008 Stena started accepting foot passengers on the ship for the first time, news that coincided with a plan to slow down the HSS *Stena Explorer* on the Dun Laoghaire crossing by 16 minutes to save costs in the face of rising fuel prices. Four months later it was announced that the *Stena Nordica* would be transferred to the Irish Sea from her usual route between Sweden and Poland as a replacement for the *Stena Seatrader*. The ship commenced her new role on 12th November that year and in March 2009 received a £2 million refit and refurbishment. The *Stena Adventurer* too received a £3.1 million refit in readiness for the 2009 season.

New sailing times including an additional sailing from both Holyhead and Dublin Port for the *Stena Nordica* came into effect from 15th March. In tandem with the changes made to the conventional service, the HSS *Stena Explorer* was rescheduled to depart from Holyhead each day at the slightly later time of 10.25. The return from Dun Laoghaire to Holyhead was retimed to leave at 13.30.

It can be seen that the Dublin service has been progressively increased pretty much at the expense of the Dun Laoghaire operation. A decline in tourist volumes as a consequence of competition from low cost airlines and other ferry operators and, more importantly, very high fuel costs associated with operating the HSS's thirsty gas turbine, combined to force Stena Line to take action. As fuel costs soared to a peak US$147 for a barrel of crude, and the global economy went into freefall, further reductions were made with the result that by November 2008, the *Stena Explorer*'s schedules fell to just one round trip per day, except for the Christmas and New Year holiday period when the vessel double tripped.

At time of writing, the prospect of Dun Laoghaire being without a sea link with Holyhead for the first time since the Irish port was built during the first half of the 19th century seemed very real indeed.

*An impressive view of Dun Laoghaire Harbour with the HSS **Stena Explorer** discharging. (Peter Barrow)*

The **Stena Explorer** *arrives at Dun Laoghaire on her morning sailing from Anglesey. From 2008 she has been only employed, most days, on one round sailing a day on the route following the hike in worldwide oil prices. (Gordon Hislip)*

The first ship in the fleet to unveil the modernised Stena Line livery, the **Stena Adventurer** *leaves Holyhead for Dublin. (Miles Cowsill)*

6 Changes to the Isle of Wight Routes

by John Faulkner

England's largest island, the Isle of Wight, is served by three principal ferry companies. Wightlink operates a vehicle and passenger service from Lymington to Yarmouth, a passenger service from Portsmouth to Ryde Pier and a vehicular ferry service from Portsmouth to Fishbourne. Red Funnel operates two services from Southampton; a vehicle and passenger service to East Cowes and a high-speed passenger service to West Cowes. Hovertravel operates the only year-round commercial hovercraft service in the world between Southsea and Ryde.

Wightlink is currently in the midst of a £57 million investment programme on its three routes whilst there have been recent changes to Red Funnel's high-speed fleet and, in 2007, Hovertravel introduced a larger and self-built craft.

WIGHTLINK – LYMINGTON TO YARMOUTH

The old C-class passenger and vehicle ferries on the western link between Lymington and Yarmouth, the *Caedmon*, *Cenwulf* and *Cenred* were built in 1973 and had reached the point where major structural replacement would have been required to retain MCA certification for passenger carrying vessels. The slippery slope had been reached – they had to go. The controversial new Wight class vessels, the *Wight Light*, *Wight Sky* and *Wight Sun* are a development of the old design. New features are a 'garage deck' that lifts 15 cars to passenger lounge level, allowing commercial vehicles to be carried beneath cars for the first time and an open passenger deck above the lounge instead of at each end of it. The ships have a slightly asymmetric layout to dovetail with the existing berths.

The new vessels were designed to meet all EU emission standards and with no engine cooling water circulating out of the ship. The engines are shut down in port, unlike the C-class ferries, and they are more fuel-efficient, fuel consumption on the considerably heavier new ships being roughly the same as their predecessors. A Voith Schneider propeller at each end of the ferries is driven by two Volvo DM16MC engines (each 478kW at 1,800 rpm) via powder clutches and toothed drive belts. Only one engine is required to drive each propeller in the confines of the winding Lymington River. Two engines per propeller also allow the ships to continue navigating in the event of an engine failure. Auxiliary engines are four Volvo D9MG, each 225kW at 1,500 rpm providing a 415-volt three-phase supply. Only one of these units is normally used during passage with a second required to drive hydraulic ramp and deck lift systems, the third and fourth units providing back up. The low-wash hull design differs radically from the C-class. Its shape and the centrally positioned propellers (they were offset port forward and starboard aft on the C class) means that they are unable to use the old slipways as the old C class could do in the event of linkspan maintenance or failure. It was considered more important to design the hull for its principal service and adapt the slipways for the more occasional use. To this end a loading barge, effectively a floating linkspan, has been built to bridge the gap between slipway and ferry. This unit can be used at Lymington, Yarmouth or Fishbourne.

The passenger lounge is very long and surrounds the garage deck, principally along the starboard side and across the ends. The passenger capacity is 28% lower than the old ships because there are far fewer foot passengers to carry in the modern era. A passenger lift connects the main deck and the single lane mezzanine deck to the passenger lounge. Unfortunately, because of the necessity to have many half landings on the stairwells to allow passenger access at all tidal states, the lift could not be incorporated on the preferred side of the ship.

The new ships, costing a total of £26 million, were built at Brodogradiliste, Kraljevica (Croatia) and each sailed to the UK under their own power. Details of dates are listed below:

The principal differences between the new and old ferries are listed in

	WIGHT LIGHT	WIGHT SKY	WIGHT SUN
Keel laid	26th Jun 2007	13th Aug 2007	26th Jan 2008
Launched	26th Jan 2008	12th Apr 2008	28th Jun 2008
Left Croatia	15th Aug 2008	16th Sep 2008	28th Mar 2009
Arrived Solent	1st Sep 2008	1st Oct 2008	14th Apr 2009
In service	25th Feb 2009	25th Feb 2009	20th May 2009

the table below:

	C CLASS	WIGHT CLASS
Length	58	62
Beam	15.2	16
Draft	2.28	2.3
Displacement - t *	861	1503
GRT - t	773	2546
Passengers	500	360
Car capacity **	48-52	65

* loaded ** current average size cars

The loaded displacement is 75% greater than the C class and 93% of this increase was necessary to comply with modern certification regulations for ship construction. Although tests carried out by consultants BMT Seatec proved that the hull design would not create any greater wash than the old ships, a furore like no other has raged over the damage that they might do to the fragile Lymington River and its marshes. Various groups at Lymington were initially interested in physical dimensions of length, beam and draft rather than displacement, which eventually appeared to trigger the disquiet. Even new versions of the C class would weigh more than 1,400 tonnes under current regulations. Although any casual observer can see that local fishing boats and other vessels that pay no heed to the river speed restriction cause far more wash than the new ferries, some opposition to them, including pending High Court action, continued at the time of writing.

The first two new ferries lay idle for months after their delivery, the *Wight Sky* in No.2 Basin at the RN dockyard in Portsmouth, pending agreement to run them. The C-class ferry *Cenwulf* was withdrawn (in

*Perhaps the best of the old C-class ferries; the 1973-built **Cenwulf** is seen inbound in the Lymington River on 9th October 2008. The photograph was taken from the bridge of the **Wight Light**, which was undergoing trials and crew training.*

*The **St Helen**, resplendent in the latest Wightlink livery, crosses from Portsmouth to Fishbourne on 4th February 2009. This ship has carried a record seven different liveries during her 26-year life.*

*The **St Catherine** is seen laid up at the former US base at Hythe on Southampton Water on 19th September 2009. She was moved from the pier head berth to the mud berth in late July so that she could be connected to a shore electrical supply and left unmanned. This ship is now sales listed.*

*Plenty of thrust is being applied as the **Wight Light** leaves Yarmouth on 13th April 2009. Although speed-restricted in the Lymington River, the Wight class has sufficient power to make up lost time crossing the Solent. Sister vessel **Wight Sky** achieved 16 knots at one point during her delivery voyage from Croatia.*

anticipation of an early sale that fell through) on 15th November 2008 but restored to service on 22nd January 2009 when the *Caedmon's* MCA certificate expired. Faced with imminent expiry of the remaining C-class certificates the new ships were put into service on 25th February 2009, starting with the *Wight Sky* at 03.45 and *Wight Light* two hours later. The *Cenwulf* finished in the early hours of the same day whilst the *Cenred* continued to operate a back-up roll during teething troubles with the new ships until 12th March, when her MCA certificate expired. The *Wight Sun* entered service on 20th May 2009 and a full three-ship service operated during high summer.

The three C-class ferries moved to Marchwood for lay-up and were sold to Smedegaarden ship breakers at Esbjerg, Denmark, although that does not necessarily mean they will be scrapped. They were still at Marchwood in October 2009.

Modification of the Yarmouth linkspan was carried out in advance of the new ferries' introduction but the service cannot operate efficiently until the Lymington linkspan and passenger access has been replaced. Currently vehicles and passengers share access at Lymington via a temporary 'ski-ramp' adapter fitted on the old linkspan. This bottleneck is increasing turn-round times. Replacement cannot begin until Wightlink has been granted a FEPA (Fisheries and Environmental Protection Act) licence, which is issued by MFA (Marine and Fisheries Agency) and CPA (Coastal Protection Act) consent issued by the Environment Agency. These bodies consult with and take note of the comments of Natural England, who remained uncommitted at the time of writing (October 2009). The modifications would only take place during the low season because the ferries would have to use the old slipway at Lymington, via the loading barge, for an 11-week period. Turn-round times are likely to be prejudiced further during reconstruction by the even less convenient docking procedures and the need to obtain an occupation of the railway line that vehicles would have to cross to gain access to and from the ferries.

WIGHTLINK - PORTSMOUTH TO RYDE

The passenger route between Portsmouth and Ryde was the principal artery to the Isle of Wight before the boom in the motor car and personal mobility. The last of the traditional ferries were replaced by a pair of bespoke Incat catamarans in 1986. Increasing age and unreliability of these ferries led to the augmentation of the fleet with a pair of four-year-old Kvaerner-built catamarans in 2000. These ferries, renamed *FastCat Shanklin* and *FastCat Ryde*, as well as being thirstier on fuel, were not ideally suited to the route due to poorer manoeuvrability and the inability for both gangways at each terminal to be used. The first of the catamarans, *Our Lady Patricia*, was withdrawn in May 2006, leaving her sister, *Our Lady Pamela*, operating principally a relief role. She ran her last services on 7th May 2009 and was sold to Smedegaarden ship breaking yard at Esbjerg, Denmark.

The financial performance of the Portsmouth to Ryde route is marginal, with some services seeing very little patronage but Wightlink has invested in the route to ensure its continuance. A pair of bespoke catamarans, designed by BMT Nigel Gee Ltd and built at FBMA in the Philippines, entered service on 29th September 2009. Named *Wight Ryder I* and *Wight Ryder II* and each powered by two Caterpillar C32 970kW engines, they are slower than the displaced craft, but far more economic. The following table provides comparisons between the three types of craft.

	RYDER	INCAT	K Class
Length	40	29.6	40
Beadth	12	11.8	10.1
Draft	1.6	2.2	1.7
Passengers	260	395**	361
Service Speed	26.9	29	34
Max Speed -kn	21	26	30
Fuel Con* -1/hr	496	700	1024
Propulsion	Screws***	Screws	Jets

* at maximum speed ** originally 470 *** Wight Ryders also with bow thrusters

The lower passenger capacity (accommodated on a single deck) is a reflection of the ongoing decline in the number of people travelling without a car. A welcome feature, not seen for over 20 years, is an accessible open deck with seating for 40 people. 'Severn Link', a company intending to operate new services between Ilfracombe and Swansea plus Minehead and Penarth, has first refusal on purchase of the Kvaerner class ferries.

The revamp of the passenger ferry route includes new berths and facilities at both terminals, with berth 2, at the eastern end of Ryde Pier, becoming the new stopping point.

WIGHTLINK - PORTSMOUTH TO FISHBOURNE

The car ferry route between Portsmouth and Fishbourne is the busiest on the Solent and it too is intended to receive a major investment. The single linkspans at the terminals produce a bottleneck that leads to substantial delays during busy periods. Clearly there is a need for change. The intention is to provide a second linkspan at a higher level for cars only. The newest and largest ferry, the *St Clare* (2001), already has a fixed high level car deck, currently accessed from the main deck via a single lane ramp, which causes more delays to the schedule than any other feature of the route. Only superficial modifications would be required to allow her to use a second linkspan.

The youngest two of the four Saint class vessels would be lengthened by 12 metres and a high-level car deck would stretch the entire length of the ship and through the current passenger lounge. A new passenger lounge, fabricated from aluminium alloy, would be built above and extend to the stern. This modification would substantially spoil the appearance of the ships, but at £5 million per ship it was considered cost effective compared to new builds. The modification would be more straightforward than that carried out to the Red Funnel Raptor class ferries as the ships would not be cut into three large pieces. Instead, a simple hull insert would be placed close to the stern, with few severed services to reconnect. The ships are getting old, the *St Faith* was built in 1990 and *St Cecilia* in 1987, but their structures, most importantly their hulls, are in very good condition. Another advantage with modifying this type of vessel, although it did not appear to have a bearing on the decision-making process, is that current ship evacuation requirements would not allow ships like these, with single central stair wells, to be built today. A very high proportion of the main deck space is made over for vehicle stowage compared to ships with stairwells on both sides.

Only one of the two original Saint class vessels, the *St Catherine* or *St Helen* (July and November 1983) would be retained, albeit with mezzanine decks removed and used principally for shipping commercial vehicles during peak periods.

It is now looking unlikely that the ship stretching plans will be implemented, eventual ship replacement becoming a preferred option.

*A never-to-be-repeated scene at the Wightlink moorings in Portsmouth Harbour on 25th June 2009. The smaller car ferry, **Wight Light**, was on her first visit to Portsmouth, being moored there for four days during fender replacement at Lymington. Beyond her is the withdrawn passenger catamaran Our Lady Pamela, which was towed away on 5th July. The large ferry, **St Clare** was taking her twice weekly refuelling stop. The fuel storage tank facility, alongside the other catamaran, **FastCat Shanklin**, was introduced a couple of years ago and obviates the need for a bunker barge to call each time a ferry requires fuelling.*

*The new Portsmouth to Ryde catamarans **Wight Ryder I** (right) and **Wight Ryder II** sit at the hulk moorings in Portsmouth Harbour on 28th July 2009. Personnel can just be made out in the wheelhouse of the 'Ryder II', which went out on trials later in the day.*

The **Wight Sun** leaves Yarmouth at 07.00 on 31st May 2009. The shell doors in the ship's sides for foot passenger access are less obtrusive than on the old C class ships. The three doors, on different levels, are barely visible between the G and L of WIGHTLINK.

The **FastCat Shanklin** approaching Ryde Pier on 26th September 2009, three days before her (scheduled) withdrawal from service.

Brought out of lay-up for the day to assist with clearing the IW Festival exodus, the **St Catherine** *approaches Fishbourne for her final time at 16:45 on 15th June 2009 as sister* **St Helen** *recedes. After she left she exchanged blasts with the inbound* **St Clare** *as if to say goodbye.*

Red Funnel's vehicle and passenger ferry **Red Osprey** *sporting an all-over IKEA advert and a 'red nose' leaving East Cowes on 15th March, the day after 'Red Nose Day, 2009'. The advertisement will be worn until her next refit, early in 2010.*

A good comparison shot of the new **Wight Ryder I** *berthed alongside the* **FastCat Ryde**, *one of the vessels she is replacing, at Portsmouth on 4th October 2009. The new vessel was off service with teething troubles.* (Andrew Cooke)

Red Funnel's newly acquired **Red Jet 5** *about to swing on to Fountain Pier on the Friday of Cowes Week 2009, nine days after she entered service.*

Meanwhile, one of the existing ferries has been taken out of service. This was mainly due to the economic downturn but in part due to the temporary loss of an overnight berth at Portsmouth owing to reconstruction of the passenger ferry berth. The *St Catherine* was chosen for no other reason than that she was due to receive her annual refit last. She was laid up at Hythe on Southampton Water on 9th April 2009, but her passenger certificate was extended for two months and she remained on standby. She subsequently saw two periods of use; two weeks from 22nd April to 6th May, when the *St Clare* was undergoing engine repairs, and three round trips on 15th June, the last day of her passenger certificate, when she helped clear the IW Festival exodus. She was offered for sale in autumn 2009.

Meanwhile, a new ticket office, reception area and cafeteria has been built at Fishbourne at the side of the marshalling area, near where it used to be prior to 1972, instead of in the centre of it. Modifications to the ferry berths, required to dovetail with modified or replacement tonnage would require the same approvals as at Lymington, but opposition on the eastern route is less intense than at Lymington.

RED FUNNEL

There have been no physical changes to Red Funnel's car ferry fleet but its original pair of catamarans, *Red Jets 1 & 2*, have left the fleet. The two craft, built at Cowes in 1991, were sold to Caspian Mainport for further service on the Caspian Sea and left Southampton aboard the freighter La Rochelle, bound for St Petersburgh, on 15th May 2009.

Their places have been taken by the timely availability of a second-hand craft designed by FBM at Cowes but built by Pequot River Shipworks, New London, Connecticut, USA in 1999. Similar in design to the Cowes-built

Red Jet 3 of 1998, but largely with different equipment and machinery and also incorporating a small, covered outer deck area astern of the wheelhouse, she was previously named *Bo Hengy* and served in the Bahamas. Replaced by a larger vessel, she was sold to Red Funnel and arrived at Southampton aboard the freighter CEC Meadow on 11th June 2009. The following day she was towed to Portchester for refit, which included internal refurbishment in line with the larger, Tasmanian-built *Red Jet 4* of 2003. Re-christened *Red Jet 5* by the Olympic gold medallist Shirley Robertson OBE in a ceremony at Cowes on 21st July, she entered service on 29th July.

HOVERTRAVEL

Hovertravel, which operates a hovercraft service between Ryde and Southsea, introduced a larger craft in June 2007 to join its two of AP.1-88/100 craft. The hull of the BHT-130 craft was fabricated by Aluminium Shipbuilders at Fishbourne, IW, and towed to Bembridge Harbour for fitting out by Hoverwork, a sister company of Hovertravel. Named *Solent Express,* she is a bespoke, passenger-only variant of a British designed BHT-130 craft built in Seattle for service in Alaska. Retired senior members of BHC staff assisted Hoverwork in design and construction of the new craft. The 131-seat craft is powered by two MTU 12V2000-R1237K37 lift engines, each 675kW, and two MTU 16V2000-R1637K37 propulsion engines, each 899kW (all air-cooled diesels), via two 3.5m diameter, five-bladed, variable pitch ducted propellers, giving a service speed of 45 knots.

The Gibraltar-based Bland Group, which owned 25 per cent of Hovertravel from 1968 took a controlling interest in the Company from April 2008.

Hovertravel's newest craft, the stylish **Solent Express,** *is seen approaching Southsea on 18th March 2009.*

7 Photo Feature - Ostend & Zeebrugge
by Mike Louagie

Two competitors on Ostend roads: the **Primrose** *and* **Phocine***.*

On 3rd May 1987, the **Prinses Paola** was caught by a force 9 north-easterly wind; the worst direction for entry into the port of Ostend. The elegant passenger-only ferry did not have any bow thrusters and had to swing in front of the harbour to enter the port stern first. During this manoeuvre she was blown in between the pier heads, providing a spectacular show but fortunately without any damage.

The **Prinses Paola** was probably the most elegant ferry ever built for the Ostend-Dover service. She is seen here entering Ostend stern first in the evening light of May 1987, her last season. On 1st April 1988, she left Ostend as the **Tropicana** and after a conversion into a cruise ship she commenced casino trips out of Miami, Florida.

*The **Free Enterprise VII** leaving Zeebrugge bound for Dover in 1987, the year when the name Townsend Thoresen disappeared following the **Herald of Free Enterprise** disaster.*

*The **Princesse Marie-Christine** in May 1988, with her new P&O livery. However, it was always difficult to hide the orange paint of the previous Townsend Thoresen era.*

The **Reine Astrid** in her spotless Oostende Lines livery shortly after a winter overhaul. In those days without the assistance of Photoshop it was always better to take photos immediately after dry-docking!

This quite unique picture shows the three sister ships together in Ostend on 27th February 1995. From left to right: the **Prins Albert**, **Prinses Maria-Esmeralda** (shortly afterwards to be renamed as **Wisteria**), and **Princesse Marie-Christine**.

After an almost political decision to halt commercial co-operation with P&O and enter into a partnership with Sally Line, the RMT fleet was repainted in 'Oostende Lines' livery and moved from Dover to Ramsgate. The Boeing Jetfoil **Prinses Stephanie** *is seen at full speed.*

The **Prinses Maria-Esmeralda** *and* **Reine Astrid** *in Ostend. Special police forces are lowered onto the deck of the* **Reine Astrid**, *via a Puma helicopter, to rescue her from an imaginary hijack.*

The French freight company Schiaffino had been fighting to establish itself in the state-owned RMT dominated port of Ostend. Their ships were only allowed to have a berth behind the Demey locks, making the crossing to Ramsgate unnecessarily long. Seen here is the **Merchant Victor** *entering Ramsgate in the early nineties.*

Once the pride of the Ostend ferry community, the **Prins Filip** *was humiliated in a freight only mode on the Zeebrugge-Dover link as the* **P&OSL Aquitaine** *(1999).*

*After the closure of the RMT service, a new start was given by Holyman Sally, with the introduction of two Incat 81-metre fast ferries, the **Holyman Diamant** (seen here in 1997), and the **Holyman Rapide**.*

*When the RMT service was closed, all their ships were sold. For redundant seafarers it came as a smack in the face to see their old ships operating again with foreign crews. Seen here is the former **Prins Albert** as the **Eurovoyager** in a short lived (1998) Sally Freight livery.*

*A scenic evening picture taken on the western pier in Ostend during April 2000. The **Diamant** arrives from Dover, whilst TransEuropa Ferries' **Eurovoyager** sails for Ramsgate.*

*The veteran ferry **Laburnum**, ex **Free Enterprise V**, made a surprise appearance at Ostend in 2001, after years on the Italy-Albania run. Too small for the service, and uneconomic because of her high-grade fuel, she was quickly withdrawn.*

*Is this a ferry museum? A pleasant morning view of Ostend in August 2001 with, from left to right: the **Laburnum**, **Primrose**, **SuperSeaCat One**, and **Roseanne**.*

*Yet another Channel workhorse is the former **Sally Sky**, seen here as **Larkspur** on the Ostend-Ramsgate service. The picture was taken from the beach at Ostend in November 2007, when a strong swell was running.*

The **Superfast X** *arriving in Zeebrugge, after a fuel-thirsty crossing from Rosyth.*

*This view, taken from a helicopter shows Ferryways' **Flanders Way** leaving the port of Ostend in April 2004.*

*It has been quite common to see ferries from Dunkirk or Calais being diverted to Ostend or Zeebrugge when fishermen blocked the French ports. An unusual visitor to Ostend was the **SeaFrance Nord Pas-de-Calais** in 2000.*

The **Balmoral** *unexpectedly berthed in Antwerp in January 2009, seeking shelter after having sailed in heavy weather in the Bay of Biscay.*

Perhaps Norfolkline's more economic **Scottish Viking** *will be able to succeed where the Superfast service failed. She is seen passing the Zeebrugge windmills bound for Scotland in July 2009.*

8 Notable Cruise Ship Withdrawals

by William Mayes

A combination of requirements in order to comply with the changes to SOLAS in 2010 and the general economic gloom has led to the withdrawal from passenger service of many older ships. The writer has selected four of those on which he has travelled.

QUEEN ELIZABETH 2

The *Queen Elizabeth 2* was launched in 1967 by HM Queen Elizabeth II. The ship's builders, Upper Clyde Shipbuilders, delivered her in December 1968, but a number of problems caused the curtailment of her inaugural cruise and the ship was returned to the shipyard. She eventually commenced her maiden voyage in May 1969, sporting a revolutionary single thin black funnel with white casing.

In 1982 she served as a British troopship during the Falklands War, conveying troops to South Georgia, and following her return she was given a major refit, from which she emerged with a light grey hull and traditional Cunard funnel colours. This hull colour lasted for only a short time and she soon reverted to a traditional black hull. In October 1986 she was sent to the Lloyd Werft shipyard at Bremerhaven, Germany for a six-month refit that included the replacement of her sometimes-troublesome steam turbines with a new diesel-electric propulsion system. When re-delivered in April 1987, she had a much more substantial funnel.

During her 39 years of service with Cunard she provided the traveller with a regular trans-Atlantic service, has undertaken numerous cruises in Europe and from the United States of America, and has completed many round-the-world cruises. From 2004, with the introduction of the *Queen Mary 2*, she was UK based, but still did annual world cruises and occasional trans-Atlantic crossings. In September 2005, she became the longest serving Cunarder ever. Her sale for $100 million was announced in the summer of 2007 and she sailed on her final Cunard voyage on 11th November 2008.

Her new operator is QE2 Enterprises, a UAE registered Government-owned company, part of the Nakheel Hotels Group, formed in 2008 specifically to operate the Nakheel-owned *Queen Elizabeth 2*. It is intended that eventually the ship will become a hotel, conference centre and museum at Nakheel's Palm Jumeirah development project, but with the global economic slowdown conversion plans appear to be on hold at present. At the time of writing the *Queen Elizabeth 2* was in dry dock and there is a strong possibility that she may go to Cape Town for up to 18 months.

The Mauritania Restaurant, at the forward end of Upper Deck was the former Tourist Class dining room, and until the ship's withdrawal from service was the only two-sitting restaurant.

The well-stocked library and bookshop were on the port side of the Quarter Deck.

The Queens Grill Lounge, adjacent to the Queens Grill, was a perfect venue for afternoon tea and pre-dinner drinks.

The QE2 makes a wonderful view as she berths at Greenock during her last visit to the Clyde in October 2008. (Miles Cowsill)

The order for the *Sagafjord* was placed with Forges et Chantiers de La Mediterranee at La Seyne-sur-Mer in France in September 1962 in a contract worth 100 million Norwegian Kroner. Ownership was split 60/40 between Den Norske Amerikalinje A/S (Norwegian America Line) and Oslo ship owner Leif Hoegh & Co. The *Sagafjord* left Oslo on her first trans-Atlantic crossing on 2nd October 1965 and a month later began a series of cruises from New York.

By 1975, Norwegian America Line was considering a sale of the ship due to her high operating costs and in October 1976 she was laid up at Norfolk, Virginia. She was back in service in April 1977 with a slightly increased passenger capacity. Two years later plans were drawn up to lengthen her but this never happened.

The ship's liner role had ceased by 1980 and three years later she was sold to Cunard Line Ltd without a change of name. She continued to operate under the name of Norwegian America Cruises for some years but was later marketed as a Cunard Line ship, although retaining her original name.

In 1996 she was chartered to Transocean Tours as the *Gripsholm* but suffered damage due to grounding and was withdrawn from service. She was acquired by Saga Shipping in October 1996 and refitted to become the *Saga Rose*. She entered service for Saga in May 1997.

In late 2006 the ship underwent her final major internal refit. Saga indicated at that time that the ship would not remain in service with the company beyond 2010 but surprisingly, during the summer of 2008 announced the retirement of the *Saga Rose* a year early. She completes her service with Saga in December 2009 and is expected to become a floating hotel, possibly in London's Docklands.

The outstanding Britannia Lounge is one of the most attractive lounges on any ship, and provides a perfect venue for afternoon tea and classical recitals.

*The **Saga Rose** preparing to depart for a cruise on 17th September 2009, during the period of the Southampton Boat Show. (John Hendy)*

The North Cape Bar is the only bar in the forward part of the ship and thus serves as the bar for the Britannia Lounge too.

The Reception is usually the first space seen on boarding at a turnaround port.

In 1969 the Deutsche-Atlantik Line of Hamburg, Germany took delivery of its largest and last ship, the *Hamburg*, from Howaldtswerke-Deutsche Werft's Hamburg shipyard. As built, she carried 790 passengers on the company's service between Cuxhaven and South America. She had a gross tonnage of 23,500 and was served by a crew of 340.

In 1973, following the withdrawal of her running mate, she took that ship's name, so was renamed *Hanseatic*. However, later that year she was laid up after her owners ran into financial difficulties. In 1974 she was acquired by SOVCOMFLOT and renamed *Maksim Gorkiy* for service with the Black Sea Shipping Company of Odessa. She was chartered during the same year for use as the 'Britannic' in the film Juggernaut.

In 1988 she underwent a major modernisation by Lloyd Werft at Bremerhaven, but while on a cruise in June of the following year almost sank after sailing into drifting ice off Spitzbergen. Passengers and crew took to the boats after the pressure of the ice on the hull caused leaks and the ship began to sink. With the assistance of the Norwegian Coastguard the hull was patched and eventually the ship was towed to an inlet to allow more thorough repairs to be carried out. About two weeks later she arrived under her own power at Bremerhaven for permanent repairs. In 1991 she was renamed slightly as the *Maxim Gorkiy*.

The ship was a long-term member of Phoenix Reisen's chartered fleet, and served that company well for almost 20 years, before being withdrawn from that company's service in November 2008 on the grounds of high operating costs. A charter had been agreed between her owner and a newly revived Orient Lines but due to the economic downturn the charter did not materialise and despite efforts to save the ship as a tourist attraction for Hamburg, she was beached at Alang on 24th February 2009 under the

The Volga Bar was a long room on the starboard side of the main public room deck and appeared to be largely original in decor and furniture.

name *Maxim M*.

The name '*Maxim Gorkiy*' was the pseudonym of the writer Aleksei Peshkov (1868-1936).

*The **Maxim Gorkiy**, operating for German tour operator Phoenix Reisen, is seen in Flam while on her last Northern Europe cruise in September 2008.*

The Rossia Lounge was one of two main entertainment rooms and was often the venue for afternoon tea.

The Odessa Restaurant was one of three dining rooms, which between them accommodated all of the passengers, thus allowing for leisurely single-sitting dining.

Fred. Olsen first started to offer what might now be regarded as proper cruises in 1966 with the arrival from Lubecker Flender-Werke at Lubeck, Germany, of the dual purpose *Black Watch* and *Black Prince*. The latter ship carried the yard number 561.

The first of this pair, was ordered jointly by Fred. Olsen and Bergen Line to serve the latter company's North Sea trades in the summer under the name *Jupiter* and to begin a new era for the Olsen's by offering cruises to the Canary Islands from London in the winter as the *Black Watch*. The impressive vehicle deck space was occupied on the northbound leg by Canary Islands fruit, destined for the tables of Northern Europe. Olsen ordered the second ship for their own account and she initially served as the *Black Prince* on Olsen's services between Harwich and Kristiansand and Amsterdam and Kristiansand in summer and joined her sister on the Canary Islands service in winter. However, in 1970 the company entered into a similar arrangement with the Bergen Line and she became the *Venus* in summer and the *Black Prince* in winter.

The arrangement between Olsen and the Bergen Line came to an end in 1986 and the *Black Watch* became the property of the latter. Fred. Olsen retained the *Black Prince* and had her converted for full cruise ship operation by Wartsila at Turku in Finland, principally by means of the installation of 125 cabins on her vehicle deck. Following her refit she was equipped with a retractable 'marina' that could be put out from the stern when at anchor for the provision of a number of sporting activities. Her refit had been designed to attract a younger and more active passenger but this was not very successful and the ship was withdrawn from cruise service.

An attempt to employ her on a new ferry service between Copenhagen and Gothenburg was a spectacular failure, primarily because her Philippine registry and international crew had caused trouble with local trades unions. She was re-fitted again, but for a British middle-aged market this

*The **Black Prince** features a small, but attractively decorated library, adjacent to the upper level of the two-tier show lounge.*

time and has been an enormous success, with a fiercely loyal following.

The ship's withdrawal was announced in 2008, and in May 2009 her sale to Servicios Acuaticos de Venezuela was confirmed, although quite what type of service she will see in the future is unknown. Her new owner operates predominantly in the offshore oil and gas industry but has also indicated an interest in setting up a Venezuelan cruise operation. The *Black Prince* was withdrawn from service in the autumn of 2009, and is unlikely to be replaced until there are signs of an upturn in the UK economy. This was the second ship in the Fred. Olsen fleet to carry the name.

Edward, Prince of Wales (1330-1376), famous for leading the victories at the battles of Crecy and Poitiers, became known as the Black Prince due to his wearing of black armour.

*Fred. Olsen Cruise Lines' **Black Prince** at Portree. (John Hendy)*

*The 11,209 gross ton **Black Prince** has served her owners well for 43 years. Parts of the elegant, wood-panelled Aquitaine Lounge at the forward end of Lounge Deck almost certainly date from the time that the ship was delivered in 1966.*

The Royal Garter Restaurant is one of two dining rooms on Lounge Deck, separated by the galley and linked by a pleasant, wide corridor on the starboard side of the ship.

9 Harwich International Cruise Port
by Stephen Brown

It may surprise some to know that cruising from Harwich, as in Parkeston Quay, was once a successful activity for the London and North Eastern Railway between 1932 and 1939. During this time the luxurious Harwich Parkeston Quay to Hook of Holland vessel *Vienna* (4,227 gross tons) was running summer season weekend trips that left on a Friday night for various ports in Holland, Belgium or France before arriving back on Monday morning. There was sometimes the added novelty of a 'mystery trip' though this usually meant sailing to the Channel Islands.

Railway ship cruising later reappeared at Harwich in the 1960s and early 1970s when the port's British Rail classic passenger ferry *Avalon* (6,584 gross tons) was used for a number of mini-cruises to Amsterdam and then full scale cruises that ranged from the northern delights of Scandinavia and the North Cape down to the much warmer southern climes of Portugal, Spain and North Africa. These proved highly popular and her spacious and luxurious accommodation was utilised mainly as 'something for the ship to do' as she was then a spare vessel at the port.

However, real cruising is traditionally done on board purpose-designed vessels to which Harwich is not historically known to have received many visitors. One notable arrival from way back was Bergen Line's *Stella Polaris* from 1927. Designed in the style of a private yacht with the on board features of an ocean liner, her distinctive style could still be seen at Harwich over 25 years later.

Yet it is only within the past 20 years or so that cruise ships, stylish or otherwise, have begun arriving in any great numbers and from today's perspective, the early arrivals were very much representative of a former era. In 1987 the *Argonaut* (4,007 gross tons and built in 1929), called in and brought with her an engaging mix of Mediterranean-style chaos and (dis)order as passengers and their baggage were literally landed on the quayside.

More formal arrangements were on hand for when the *Jupiter* (9,499 gross tons) did a one-off visit in 1990 followed by others being seen more often such as Chandris Lines who, in 1991 with the *Azur* (11,609 gross tons) and then in 1992 with the 1936-built *Victoria* (14,917 gross tons) ran a series of cruises to the North Cape, Spitzbergen and the Baltic.

A WISE DECISION

The foundation for the present day importance of Harwich International Port as a major cruise terminal (the port changed its name in 1997) dates from 1993 when a decision was made to diversify into cruising proper and add to its already established status as a major ferry port. By emphasising its location, just 50 miles from London Stansted airport and only 70 minutes by rail from London itself, with trains running from a station directly alongside the quay, it was thought it already possessed the infrastructure and facilities required to act as a 'turnround port' i.e. as a terminal for cruise passengers either joining or leaving the ship as opposed to 'transit' where ships call in en-route with passengers/tourists who visit.

With open access onto the North Sea, the target markets for any new arrivals and departures would be those of Northern Europe and Scandinavia during a season that would run from May to September. The advantage of this to the operators was that it offered an alternative area of deployment and source of income for their ships away from the frequently overcrowded Caribbean and Mediterranean.

Throughout 1993, Harwich played host to the *Columbus Caravelle* (7,560 gross tons), the *Funchal* (9,563 gross tons) and the *Russ* (12,800 gross tons) together with the arrival of perhaps the most inspirational of the early operators, Royal Caribbean Cruise Line (RCCL). Their *Song of Norway* (23,000 gross tons) and *SunViking* (18,600 gross tons) ran a total of 14 cruises to various places within Norway and throughout the Baltic and a subsequent commitment by RCCL to then base their operations at Harwich became the catalyst that convinced the port it had made the right decision.

As a consequence of RCCL's move, one of the earliest jobs was to paint up the nearest of the container terminal cranes from an old and peeling yellow to a more maritime style of blue that better matched RCCL colours. Celebrity status arrived when one of the company's regular cruisers, comedian Ernie Wise, was seen during a ship visit.

THE FIRST BIG ONE

The first truly big cruise ship to visit Harwich, and the largest ship the port had then seen, was Crystal Cruises' *Crystal Harmony* (49,400 gross tons). This white giant of a ship docked at No.1 berth on the morning of 7th June 1994 during what was termed 'Cruise Day'. She had arrived following a trans-Atlantic voyage from New York and left the same day for the Baltic. Further up the quay was berthed a now somewhat diminutive looking *Song of Norway*.

Ships visiting during 1995 included the *Vistafjord* (24,292 gross tons) and the *Black Prince* (11,209 gross tons) yet throughout all the expanding business the situation remained that berths and facilities at the port were still very much those that greeted passengers from the day-to-day ferries. It was further realised, due to the increasingly large size of ships that were coming on stream and might visit if suitable facilities were on offer, that something major had to be done to improve matters. Paint jobs were no longer enough, a bold initiative was needed if the port was to step up a gear.

NEW FACILITIES

It was therefore decided to construct a purpose-built embarkation hall, just for cruise passengers, towards the eastern end of the quay and to dedicate No. 1 berth for super-sized cruise ships. It was all to be built within easy access of the adjacent railway station and completed by May 1996 at a cost of £1 million. This new hall featured a 200-seat lounge, complete with quality refreshment facilities, plus 20 check-in desks to enable passengers to speed through the embarkation formalities. Parking and drop-off areas were created close by for up to 60 coaches and 400 cars together with a dedicated baggage handling system. Being all white it was somewhat unfavourably compared to

*The St Nazaire-built **Royal Princess** was originally the **R Eight** before becoming the **Minerva II** in 2003. In 2007 she was transferred to Princess Cruises. (Harwich International Port)*

*The **Costa Atlantica** was built in Helsinki during 2000. During the winter months she cruises in the Caribbean. (Harwich International Port)*

that of a DIY warehouse whilst locally it was nicknamed 'the shed'. However, it was a step in the right direction.

The berth and approach channel had already been dredged to accommodate vessels with a draught of up to 9.5 metres at all states of the tide whilst, with a view to the future, there was no limit placed on the width or length of ship that could tie up there. At the time it was thought that ships up to 300 metres long and 85,000 gross tons would be about the maximum size expected though rumours that ships of up to 135,000 gross tons might arrive were not denied. Were they correct? Well, almost.

GROWTH

Over the intervening years growth has greatly exceeded all initial expectations. The lead operator RCCL has since positioned some of its largest ships at Harwich, the first being in 1996 when the *Splendour of the Seas* (69,130 gross tons) arrived and there remained a regular each year until the end of the 2000 season. Her sheer size, when compared to the port's earlier visitors, was simply astonishing especially as she dwarfed the old station hotel behind which it was often impossible, in earlier days, to see even if a North Sea ferry was lying alongside! The 1997 season saw a total of 23 cruise ship visits including the *Ocean Majesty* (10,417 gross tons), the *Aegean 1* (11,563 gross tons) and the *Funchal* with the highlight being a one-off courtesy call by the 280-metre long *Enchantment of the Seas* (74,136 gross tons), then the longest vessel to have berthed at Harwich International Port. The total number of passengers that year was 54,000.

By April 1998 a further £500,000 had been spent on improving the terminal by further extending it an extra 50% in order to provide a new reception and check-in area plus a larger baggage handling facility. Seating was now for 300 passengers and the parking increased to 600 cars and coaches. That same year saw 31 visits although the choice of operator was still not huge – the *Ocean Majesty* was booked to call 13 times! RCCL made another one-off visit with their *Vision of the Seas* (78,491 gross tons) as overall passenger numbers showed a slight year-on-year increase at 55,700.

Matters improved dramatically during 1999 with 49 visits that included new customers, Holland America Line with their *Maasdam* (55,451 gross tons) and *Rotterdam* (59,652 gross tons) in addition to Royal Olympic's *Odysseus* (9,639 gross tons). Passenger throughput jumped to 77,385.

MORE CHOICE

Thereafter an ever-widening choice of ships and operators varied the size and style of cruises that were available. Small ships, that could navigate small fjords and ports, and large ships, that would visit major Baltic capitals, were all welcomed in increasing numbers, the range including the old and the new, traditional and glitzy, the cheap, cheerful and not so cheap. Favourites returned such as the *Funchal* and the *Van Gogh* (16,330 gross tons) plus one that was never a cruise ship to start with but a converted cargo liner, now the *Princess Danae* (17,074 gross tons). Meanwhile the big got ever bigger. The *Brilliance of the Seas* (90,090 gross tons) was RCCL's regular ship for the 2002 season only to be replaced by the slightly smaller *Grandeur of the Seas* (74,137 gross tons) in 2003.

In 2002 Airtours arrived with the *Sundream* (no stranger to the port being the former *Song of Norway*) making several trips whilst August that year saw one-off visits first from the *Constellation* (90,228 gross tons) followed the day after by the *Carnival Legend* (85,920 gross tons).

Subsequent years were to see one-offs turn into regulars. The *Discovery*

Built as a steam ship in 1961, the classic Portuguese cruise ship **Funchal** *has been a regular visitor to Harwich. (John Hendy)*

New in 2009, the **Costa Luminosa** *was built by Fincantieri in Venice. (Harwich International Port)*

Holland America's **Eurodam** *is the lead ship of the 'Signature' class and was named by Queen Beatrix of the Netherlands. (Harwich International Port)*

(21,186 gross tons) has been making repeat calls since 2003 whilst the *Ocean Majesty* seems never to have been away. The resident RCCL ship since 2005 has been the *Jewel of the Seas* (90,090 gross tons) whilst Thomson Tours replaced the *Sundream* firstly with the *Thomson Celebration* (33,930 gross tons) and then with the *Thomson Spirit* (37,773 gross tons).

Not only do the regulars return each year but they also make up the bulk of the yearly sailings as only three or four ships might each do 10 to 12 trips per season. It is a fitting testament to how satisfied those operators are with the port's arrangements and it acts as an inducement for others, so much so that on several occasions there have been three cruise ships berthed alongside at once using suitably equipped other berths. The number of calls each year has steadied at between 45 and 55 though rising to 61 in 2007, a year which saw the *MSC Lirica* (59,058 gross tons) visit and reaching a high of 70 in 2008, during which the sister to the 'Lirica', the *MSC Opera* arrived. The total number of cruise passengers that year was 133,660.

However, the recent economic downturn meant that 2009 slipped back to just 53 booked visits though amongst the list were three impressive Costa vessels; the *Costa Magica* (105,000 gross tons), *Costa Atlantica* (85,619 gross tons) and *Costa Luminosa* (92,700 gross tons) in addition to Holland America's *Eurodam* (86,000 gross tons), each making transit or inaugural visits. The *Costa Magica* was, in May 2006, the first ever to break the 100,000 gross ton mark after having been diverted, at very short notice, from her booked call at Dover due to bad weather.

LOCAL BENEFIT

One spin off common to all major cruise ports is the anticipation of a boost to local trade from the visiting passengers and crew and thus businesses, both commercial and tourist based, have since sought to showcase 'Olde Harwich'.

Unfortunately the majority of cruise passengers still use Harwich principally as their embarkation point after having either flown into the UK, largely from America, or having travelled from elsewhere within the UK by road or dedicated 'cruise-trains' to and from London.

This means that the local attractions are often lost on those who prefer to spend time 'freshening up' or 'using the facilities' on board. However, the port is having increasing success at attracting more transit calls and so for those travelling on a tour, a series of guided walks around the ancient and historic town, arranged by the local Harwich Society, are a welcome and informative leg stretch. Tours are also arranged to visit nearby picturesque Constable Country or to places of cultural interest such as Cambridge.

For the local townsfolk, just seeing the cruise ships is a major attraction in themselves with the town's Ha'penny Pier often full of well wishers watching them leave on many a summer's evening. It's well known for day visitors also to arrive just to watch those departures, (most leave at 17.00) and yearly guides detailing when the ships are due are available on the port's website at www.harwich.co.uk

BOOK IT

The idea of a cruise from Harwich remains one to be highly recommended and operators should remain attracted to a port fully able to meet the demands of the industry through its own flexibility and adaptability. There is literally a cruise on offer that appeals to everyone from those preferring a sedate and older clientele-focused fjord trip in early season right through to the younger or young at heart who like a more cosmopolitan 'floating city at sea' style cruise complete with atriums and on-deck golf courses.

That decision taken back in 1993 has been amply rewarded in that operators such as Celebrity Cruises, Royal Caribbean, Holland America, Carnival Cruises, Voyages of Discovery, Page and Moy and Thomson were all to become regular users. In doing so they gave a new variation to the old slogan of 'Harwich for the Continent'.

In future years that list will no doubt vary and evolve and whilst some may leave, others will arrive to replace them. So far the longest ship to berth is the *Constellation* at 294 metres. Time will tell if that rumoured ship of 300 metres or 135,000 gross tons finally arrives but in the meantime Harwich International Port will continue to pursue its vision of being 'the port of first choice'.

Dressed overall, the **Jewel of the Seas** *is seen alongside during May 2009. (John Bryant)*

10 Soviet Russia's 'Author' Class

by David Trevor-Jones

The Soviet Black Sea Shipping Company placed its order for three of a new class of 20,000 gross ton liners with V.E.B. Mathias Thesen Werft in Wismar, then in East Germany, early in 1962. A second batch of three was ordered in Spring 1964. The yard had completed a stylish small cruise ship for the East German trades unions, the *Fritz Heckert*, in 1961 and the new ships for the Soviet fleet were to be similarly modern in style. Their centrally placed raked funnel, streamlined mast, balanced superstructure and pronounced sheer presented a racy profile, generically similar to that of the roughly contemporaneous *Sagafjord*. An unusual feature was the drawing of the elegant stern into a sharp reverse prow.

DESIGN

The hull and superstructure designs were the result of extensive experimental tank testing and were considered to represent the optimum in scientific hydro and aerodynamic design. Just as their operator's perception of them was as products of the latest technological advances, to western shipping observers and passengers they bristled with science. The author remembers being immediately intrigued by the forest of aerials festooning the upper works of the *Mikhail Lermontov* when first inspecting her as an eager young cruise passenger. Their hulls were ice strengthened to 'following a breaker in broken ice' class.

The late 1960s and 70s was the coolest period of the cold war. Among the prospective deployments for these multi-role ships were line voyaging and cruising, roles that would link east with west. A stated Soviet aim was a Leningrad-New York line route but the ships could equally work as troopers and were engineered to carry heavier than usual commercial deck loads as evidenced by their extremely powerful deck gear and a cruising range of in excess of 10,000 nautical miles. Their relatively spartan interior design could either be interpreted as Russian modernism or as hinting at another purpose.

The first of the first trio was handed over in October 1964. The *Ivan Franko* became the name ship for the class, exciting much interest when she called at Tilbury on her maiden voyage from Leningrad to Odessa in December. The second, the *Alexandr Puskin*, entered service in August 1965 followed by the third, *Taras Shevchenko*, in April 1967.

Only two of the second batch were built. The *Shota Rustaveli* entered service in 1968 and after an interval the fifth and last of the class, the *Mikhail Lermontov,* was delivered in 1972. In 1974 the Soviet shipping lines succeeded in purchasing the former West German merchant flagship *Hamburg*, then only five years old, via an intermediary based in the USA. Renamed *Maxsim Gorkiy* and only very slightly larger than the preceding five 'Authors' (though somewhat more luxurious) she might have taken both the place and the name of the abortive sixth Wismar ship.

The five 'Authors' were externally similar but differed slightly in their internal arrangements. Each measured nominally at 19,860 gross tons, 578

The **Ivan Franko** *arriving at Tilbury in July 1965 showing her original forward superstructure. (John Hendy)*

feet overall with a beam of 77 feet and a draft of 26 feet; service speed was nominally 20 knots with a passenger capacity of 750 (with 500 deck passengers on short trips). The first four were built with holds accommodating between 1,000 and 1,500 tons of cargo and 23 cars which were loaded through shell doors on the Second Deck.

ON BOARD

The *Ivan Franko* was powered by two Sulzer RD76 10,500 b.h.p. engines which were built in Holland by De Schelde and although the others were intended to be powered by MAN K9Zs they are listed as having also been equipped with Sulzers. The engine room was visible to passengers from a series of lights, apparently permanently propped open, atop a casing aft of the funnel on the Boat Deck.

All of the public rooms were ranged along the Saloon Deck, save for the restaurant which was on Upper Deck. At the forward end the Music Salon featured a large dance floor. Aft of it were two separate cafes to either side of a narrow and largely glazed corridor. A vestibule midships provided the 'town square' off which lay shops, a post office and kiosk. From here aft there were partial external promenades enclosing to starboard a bar, smoking saloon and games room and to port a cinema and library. Furthest aft, an indoor pool was enclosed within a solarium with an opening roof and associated bar. A second, shallower pool for children was situated on the fantail below on Promenade Deck.

As originally built, the saloon and promenade deck superstructures of the first four ships stepped forward slightly from the bridge. These were extended to accommodate expanded public room space in the early 1970s (the *Mikhail Lermontov* was built in this form), creating a deep tier below the bridge that spoiled their elegant bow quarter. It appears that the Music Salon forward on Saloon Deck was not only enlarged forward but also

The **Taras Shevchenko** *showing her modified forward superstructure and the white hull that she carried later in her career. (FotoFlite)*

The **Ivan Franko** *with her original hull colour and livery but after the extension of her forward superstructure. (FotoFlite)*

Approaching the mouth of the River Tagus at Belem (Lisbon), the **Assedo**, *was formerly the* **Shota Rustavelli***.(Luis Miguel Correia - lmcshipsandthesea.blogspot.com)*

The restaurant aboard the **Assedo** *retained its original 'Georgian' decorative elements. (David Trevor-Jones)*

The forward stair and foyer of the **Assedo***'s Saloon Deck, much as built but for its lighting. (David Trevor-Jones)*

The indoor pool and pool bar aft on the **Assedo***'s Saloon Deck. (David Trevor-Jones)*

Original décor survived on the aft bulkhead of the **Assedo***'s Music Salon. (David Trevor-Jones)*

One of the pair of cafes aft of the **Assedo** *'s Music Salon on her Saloon Deck. (David Trevor-Jones)*

Immaculate after refit but destined for the beach at Chittagong, the former **Taras Shevchenko**, *her name shortened to* **Tara** *for the voyage, passes through the Bosphorus. (Mehmet Yapici - www.fotoio.com)*

upward, at least on the *Alexandr Puskin*, as later deck plans show stairs leading from either side of the dance floor up to a new lounge on the Boat Deck. On the *Shota Rustaveli* and, in the author's recollection, on the *Mikhail Lermontov* the upper space was not linked but configured instead as a separate lounge. The latter occupied space that was occupied by cabins in the original arrangement. Compensating for that loss the all-round promenade was sacrificed. New inside cabins were created in the forward section of Promenade Deck, the only ones on the ship as originally all passenger and most crew cabins were outside. The Achilles' heel of the ships' arrangement was that few of the passenger cabins had private facilities. Bathroom blocks occupied the central cores of Main, Second and Third Decks. It was the absence of en-suite bathrooms that probably spelled the premature end for most of the class. The early refits also saw the removal of some or all of the cargo facilities and installation of stabilisers.

All five ships received further refits in the early 80s but only one, the *Mikhail Lermontov*, was brought up fully to the standards expected in the western cruise market. When re-launched in 1982 she featured private facilities throughout, new suites, reconfigured public rooms including the addition of a balcony to the Music Salon (i.e. the linking of the lower and upper forward lounges), a night club and a new outdoor pool and lido on Boat Deck.

CAREERS

The 'Author' class ships were best known to British observers and passengers as liners on the Southampton to Montreal run and as cruise ships, synonymous with the Charter Travel Club (CTC) Line. The *Aleksandr Puskin* operated line voyages from Leningrad to Canada from new until 1979 or 1980, sharing duties with the *Mikhail Lermontov* from 1972. The latter ship then inaugurated the long-planned liner route to New York in

1975.

The Charter Travel Club was founded in Sydney in 1966 'to provide transport between Australia and Europe by the most economic means possible commensurate with comfort and safety' and was launched in November 1967 with the charter of Holland America Line's *Maasdam* for a one-way voyage to Southampton. However, it seems that the CTC might also have been a Soviet 'front' as it chartered the brand new *Shota Rustaveli* for her maiden voyage outbound from Southampton to Sydney and Auckland in October 1968, returning as CTC voyage 3. The *Shota Rustaveli* remained on the Australia line voyage service and by 1973 was advertised as operated by CTC Line, as was much of the entire Soviet passenger fleet.

The *Mikhail Lermontov* entered service as a cruise ship, her maiden voyage being a 21-night cruise to West Africa departing from Tilbury on 22nd April 1972. CTC Line cruises were initially marketed in the UK by Royal Mail Lines and offered significantly lower daily rates than the established UK lines. The author's family sailed on the *Mikhail Lermontov*'s sixth cruise in August 1972, an adventure not least because of the thrill of sailing on a Russian ship at that time of enmity between the west and the eastern block. The ship was quite unlike the P&O ships of this young passenger's experience. In marked contrast with today's generic international style, it was a time when ships expressed their origins and the *Mikhail Lermontov* was emphatically Soviet.

The lounges were relatively sparsely decorated but with acres of frilled net curtains at the windows, the main forward lounge permanently in darkness as the curtains were not opened during the day. Vodka flowed freely. The food was luxurious by domestic Soviet and opulent by today's western standards with sturgeon and caviar appearing regularly, interspersed with borscht and other Russian standards. One afternoon tea memorably included small 'apple' tarts that were actually filled with cabbage!

Other indelible memories include the dark faux-mahogany formica panelling that lined almost every bulkhead, the very high step overs at every external doorway, peering into the engine room from the top lights, the forest of aerials and the complete absence of any licensing law that prohibited beer or vodka sales to teenagers! Fellow British passengers were not very different from the P&O crowd – the CTC pricing did not seem to attract a different audience but rather, perhaps a more adventurous middle-class one. It was a happy experience, culminating in the mass migration of hundreds of distinctively brass-hair dyed Soviet women from the ship into town when we docked at Tilbury (the gender equality of the crew was noticeable – early publicity for the *Shota Rustaveli* boasted that more than half of her crew were female).

Some thirty years later little had changed other than the hair-dos as the *Assedo,* (Odessa backwards) the surprisingly re-activated former *Shota Rustaveli*, sailing with Russian passengers, called at Tilbury and cohorts of tourists staggered back to their ship weighed down with bulging Marks and Spencer carrier bags. On board, the ship was still spartan by contemporary western cruise standards but characteristically 'Russian' although she was actually Ukrainian-owned by then. A vast number of bars occupied rooms with few soft furnishings and a main meeting/lounging space had fixed tables and benches as if in a discount chain pizza restaurant.

DISPOSAL

Whilst under the command of the Picton pilot, the *Mikhail Lermontov*, the only member of the class to be upgraded to modern western cruise ship standards whilst still in Soviet ownership and billed as 'the pride of the Soviet merchant marine', sank off Port Gore after hitting rocks at the entrance to Marlborough Sound, New Zealand, on 16th February 1986. One crewman was lost but the other 347 crew and all 327 cruise passengers aboard were rescued. Indecision by the ship's acting Master, who after initially grounding the sinking vessel in shallow waters, failed to drop her anchors before seeing her drift away on a rising tide, effectively sealed the ship's fate. She lies in 15 fathoms, a popular but hazardous dive site that has claimed the lives of three recreational divers.

The *Ivan Franko* disappeared from English language brochures and effectively from view through the 70s and 80s and was the first of the class to be scrapped, arriving at Alang as the *Frank* in July 1997 after languishing for two years at Ilyichevsk, Ukraine. The break up of the Soviet Union had thrown its passenger shipping into turmoil. CTC Line was a casualty, folding in 1988 after a final season in the UK cruise market with the

*The **Ivan Franko**, at the peak of her Soviet career, is pictured at Lisbon. (Luis Miguel Correia)*

Southern Cross, the former P&O *Spirit of London / Sun Princess*.

Both the *Taras Shevchenko* and *Shota Rustaveli* were also laid up at Ilyichevsk before in February 2001 the latter was reactivated and renamed *Assedo* for a three-year period. Sadly her cruises failed to attract the passengers necessary to keep her operational and with world steel prices then enjoying a boom, she was suddenly withdrawn and left her Ukrainian lay-up after de-storing on 3rd November 2003, arriving at Alang for breaking 25 days later.

The *Taras Shevchenko* was on charter to a German operator and became Ukrainian-owned on her return in 1995, reportedly rebuilt and briefly operated as a cruise ship before her arrest in Piraeus in 1998. Five years' lay-up followed until after the departure of the *Assedo*, she received an extensive refit followed by only a very brief period of operation before she was sold to Bangladeshi breakers. Renamed *Tara* for her delivery voyage, she was beached at Chittagong at the end of January 2005.

The final survivor is the second of the class, the former *Alexandr Puskin*. She was bought in 1991 by Jerry Herrod and extensively rebuilt in Greece to become the much-loved *Marco Polo*. As such she is effectively a new cruise ship of 1991 fitted into the 1964 hull. Herrod's Orient Line was taken over by the Norwegian Cruise Line in 1998 and briefly became a two-ship operation before NCL announced its closure, effective from March 2008, and sale of the *Marco Polo* to Global Maritime which has chartered her to Transocean Tours. She continues to cruise in the British as well as in the German markets.

*The unlucky **Mikhail Lermontov** was the last ship of the class and is seen in her final rebuilt form. She was lost off New Zealand in February 1986. (Luis Miguel Correia)*

*The **Alexandr Puskin** was converted and became the **Marco Polo** in 1991. As such, she is the only survivor of the quintet and is seen leaving Dover in August 2007. (John Hendy)*

11 Photo Feature - Dover
by John Mavin

Formerly the **Crystal Harmony**, *the* **Asuka II** *entered service for Asuka Cruises in 2006, replacing the original* **Asuka** *(now Phoenix Reisen's* **Amadea***).*

A history of this ship could stretch into volumes. Originally built by Fairfield's of Govan for Canadian Pacific as the **Empress of Britain**, she entered service in 1956, and her subsequent career saw her with a number of different names before finally becoming **The Topaz** in 1998. She was chartered to Peace Boat in 2003 before finally being replaced. Here she is on a visit in 2004.

Another classic ship to survive the passing of time is Classic International Cruises' **Princess Daphne**. Originally the cargo liner **Port Sydney** of 1955 and rebuilt in 1975, she has formerly sailed under the names **Daphne**, **Switzerland** and **Ocean Monarch**.

Originally entering service in 1980, and one of a class of seven similar ships built in Poland for the Black Sea Shipping Company, the **Paloma I** *(ex* **Dimitri Shostakovich**, *ex-***Paloma***) still retained her car loading ramp to enable cruise passengers' cars to be carried. She is seen here in 2005 operated by D&P Cruises. She is now the gambling ship* **Royale Star** *and based in Singapore.*

NCL's 93,000-ton **Norwegian Gem** *in October 2007. She is one of the larger vessels in the NCL fleet, which are immediately identifiable by their striking paintwork. Her sister* **Norwegian Jewel** *has replaced the* **Norwegian Dream** *on the regular Dover itinerary.*

*Just once in a while the opportunity to see two classic sisters in port together arises. Such a time was in May 2007 when the **Saga Rose** and **Saga Ruby** called at Dover.*

*Probably the ship held with most affection at Dover – the **Saga Rose**. Little needs to be said about this remarkably beautiful vessel that has frequented the port for many years. She made her final call on 8th June 2009 before embarking on her final cruises prior to retirement.*

*For just a few hours in darkness in November 2007 the former NCL ship **Norwegian Crown** called at Dover to discharge stores and fittings prior to sailing for Hamburg where she would be converted to Fred. Olsen's new flagship - a process which included lengthening her by some 30 metres. The following February she returned as the **Balmoral**.*

*Holland America Line's **Prinsendam** was formerly the **Seabourn Sun** and **Royal Viking Sun**. It was under this Cunard name that she presided over the official opening of Dover Cruise Terminal on 20th June 1996.*

Dover was chosen for the inaugural visit and naming ceremony by Sophia Loren for MSC's huge **Poesia** *in April 2008, a spectacular event that was only slightly marred by the appalling weather!*

Built by John Brown in 1966 as the **Kungsholm** *for Swedish America, the* **Mona Lisa** *has sailed under many names and during 2008/09 she sailed as the* **Peace Boat**. *The prospects are that her distinguished career will continue.*

*Although not a regular user of Dover, Royal Caribbean ships make occasional visits. This is the **Jewel of the Seas** in April 2008.*

*Another sad departure from the cruise market is the steam turbined **Maxim Gorkiy**. Her hosting of the 1989 summit talks between Presidents Bush Sr and Gobachev in Malta, her appearance in the film Juggernaut, and her near-sinking after meeting an iceberg are mere incidents in her illustrious career. Despite attempts by Wayne Heller and Orient Lines to save her, the world recession cast her onto the scrapping beaches at Alang. This image is of her final sailing from Dover in September 2008.*

The **Fram** is a 500-passenger capacity cruise ship that has been designed with a reinforced hull for cruising Arctic waters. MS **Fram** is operated by the Hurtigruten ASA Group and is registered in Norway. The ship made its first maiden voyage to Greenland in May 2007.

At 116,000 tons the **Crown Princess** is probably the largest ship to visit Dover (although Celebrity's **Constellation** is longer). Entering service in 2006 she lacks the aft-mounted 'spoiler' that is a feature of other large Princess ships.

At the smaller end of the Costa Cruises market, and bearing their characteristic 'stovepipe' funnels, is the **Costa Marina**. *Originally built in 1969 as the container ship* **Axel Johnson**, *she was converted for cruising in 1990, along with her (slightly longer) sister the* **Costa Allegra**.

Celebrity's **Constellation** *operated her summer schedule from Dover for a number of years before transferring to Harwich. Originally the main propulsion was entirely by gas turbines driving azimuth pods, she also features a steam turbine generating plant. She is seen here in 2003 in her dark blue livery dwarfing the lighthouse of the Admiralty Pier.*

Another opportunity to see two classic sisters in port together was in August 2007 with the arrival of Fred. Olsen's very popular the **Black Watch** *and* **Boudicca**. *Dating from the early 70s these Finnish-built ships of the Royal Viking class regularly operate from Dover.*

A third member of the class is the **Albatros** *owned by Phoenix Reisen.*

Not all cruise calls are major events. In September 2008 the tiny **Clipper Adventurer** called to pick up a few passengers and then sailed again - all within an hour!

A stark contrast to the huge floating hotels of the modern cruise market is the luxurious **Hebridean Princess**. Originally the 1964-built former MacBrayne ferry **Columba**, she sailed the Scottish islands until being converted for cruising in a more dignified style in 1989. Her off-season annual visits to Dover are part of a regular around Britain cruise.

Crossing the Adriatic
by John May

The Reader's Digest magazine used to run a regular feature entitled 'What's in a name?' Two names central to this part of the world are those of the pioneer car ferries on the Adriatic, *Appia* and *Egnatia*.

ANCIENT WAYS

Beside the now largely abandoned Statzione Marittima on the not entirely fragrant harbour of Brindisi in southern Italy is a set of ancient marble steps marking the end of the Roman Via Appia which connected the capital of Rome with what two millennia ago was already the main port for her provinces in Greece, Turkey and the Middle East. Beyond the sea the connection was continued along the Via Egnatia, over the mountains from the Adriatic to the Aegean Sea and on to the eastern capital of the Roman world in Constantinople – now Istanbul. The two roads were linked by sea and the connection has been maintained for the ensuing two millennia to the present. The year 2010 marks the fiftieth anniversary of modern ferries entering the service and it is appropriate to look back over the developments that have been seen in the last half century.

In the 1950s there were two leading companies on the Adriatic. The Greek flag carrier Hellenic Mediterranean Lines was established in 1939 and proved to be experts at the rebuilding of the older tonnage which was the trademark of Greek post-war shipping. Secondly there was the Italian company Adriatica, a part of the state-owned Finmare group which had been established by the dictator Mussolini in 1936 and already well provided with a fleet of post-war motor ships operating throughout the area between Venice and Egypt. In a rare demonstration of co-operation in what was and remains a fiercely competitive environment, it was agreed that a joint service would be established with vessels that would operate in tandem from Brindisi to Patras via the intermediate Greek ports of Corfu and the then little known bay of Igoumenitsa, close to the tightly sealed border with Albania.

A provincial country town connected to the rest of the country by winding mountain roads, Igoumenitsa has a natural harbour providing deep water and shelter on all sides from the wind, characteristics not shared elsewhere in north-western Greece. While offering little attraction to the passenger steamers that had previously sailed the Adriatic routes, it was chosen by the two companies as the first mainland stop for their ferries which then continued to Patras in the Peloponnese, then as now the major hub for transportation on the west coast and an important commercial centre in its own right. Significantly the distance between the terminals could be covered economically with time to reload in 24 hours so that each ship could provide three round trips per week and still have time for a rest day for vessel and crew.

EGNATIA

The first car ferry to arrive was the elegant *Egnatia*, which had been ordered from the Loire-Normandie yard in 1958 which had recently delivered the *Compiegne* to SNCF's Calais-Dover service. The two ships were near sisters in their dimensions and hull design although the Greek vessel was equipped with relatively comfortable (by the standards of the time) cabins for overnight passage and had smaller engines driving her at 18 knots, a speed which was sufficient for her service. She was initially chartered by HML from the National Tourist Organisation of Greece which had earlier taken delivery of several passenger vessels from Italian yards. These had been built as war reparations and were chartered to Aegean operators on routes designed to spread the prosperity of tourism among the population of what was then a relatively backward part of Europe. The introduction of an international car ferry was seen in the same progressive way and the revolution in society that Greece has since experienced can be partially attributed to the spread of modern ferry services.

The *Egnatia* could carry 1,400 passengers, mainly on deck but with 434 cabin berths while her car deck had space for just 130 cars, more than sufficient for the initial demand. Not only was the dream of universal car ownership still far off but Greece was a hard country for driving with scarcely 4,000 kilometres of tarred roads at the time. Although she could accommodate small buses, no freight was carried. Her passenger facilities were comfortable rather than luxurious and her catering is not remembered to have achieved much success. However, the efficient rail connection at Brindisi and the publicity that the service received ensured good carryings and the first season was a notable success in the new market.

APPIA

The following year saw the delivery of the delightful *Appia* from the Breda yard in Venice, to Adriatica – her appearance enhanced with a superb ginger brown hull colour and her funnel carrying her owner's traditional cast metal representation of the winged lion, the symbol of the medieval republic of Venice. Slightly smaller with berths for only 200, the noise of her Fiat diesels would become a familiar feature of the Adriatic for over four decades. The two ships provided six weekly departures in each direction during the summer and the pattern was followed for the rest of the decade.

The seventies and eighties saw ever expanding numbers of new companies entering the Adriatic trade, notably with a series of conversions of passenger and cargo liners from British owners which were subject to remarkable conversions in Greek shipyards. These included the former *Bloemfontein Castle* of Union-Castle which had been with Chandris Lines since 1959 as their *Patris* on liner services to Australia but was converted by her owners in 1976 into a side loading car ferry without change of name. She eventually joined the fleet of Karageorgis Lines who had previously converted the Ellerman vessels *City of Exeter* and *City of York* into the curiously styled *Mediterranean Sea* and *Mediterranean Sky*. Progressively the early generations of car ferries from northern Europe including the *Egnatia's* half-sister *Compiegne* came to the Adriatic and the remaining

Igoumenitsa in 1960 with a light load of period vehicles being loaded onto the newly delivered **Egnatia***.
(John May collection)*

Unloading the **Egnatia** *at Brindisi in 1960. (John May collection)*

The remarkable conversion of Ellerman's cargo liner **City of Exeter** *of 1953 into the Karageorgis ferry*
Mediterranean Sea *seen at speed in the mid 1970s. (John May collection)*

Built for SNCF as their **Compiegne***, the half-sister of HML's* **Egnatia** *came to the Adriatic in 1981 as
the* **Ionian Glory** *of Strintzis Lines. (John May collection)*

The **Appia** *early in her career making a call at Igoumenitsa. (John May collection)*

Adriatica's **Espresso Venezia** *of 1977 making a morning call at Corfu. (John May)*

*Thoresen's **Viking I** of 1964 joined the fleet of HML in 1991 as the **Neptunia** and is seen at speed off Corfu. The following year she was renamed as the **Media II** and remained in the fleet until 2002. (John May)*

*HML's **Egnatia** was the pioneer car ferry in the Adriatic and is seen later in her career arriving in Patras. (John May)*

*Built as the Belgian **Koningin Fabiola** in 1962, the elegant **Lydia** served HML from 1985 to 1995 and is seen leaving Corfu. (John May)*

*By the time she left HML's fleet in 1994 the **Corinthia** was the last steam turbine powered ferry in operation in Europe. She had been built for British Railways in 1956 as the **Duke of Argyll**. (John May)*

*The **Superfast XII** arriving at Patras. (John May)*

passenger vessels departed while the competition put pressure on the original pair of companies.

Hellenic Mediterranean had always given the impression of being more interested in passenger than vehicle carrying and continued to operate with elderly ships offering increasingly outdated accommodation on their services until their final sailing departed from Brindisi on 6th September 2004, operated by the chartered and particularly decrepit *Arielle*, originally a Japanese train ferry which had seen service with several Adriatic operators before her final charter to HML. During the same period Adriatica was also in decline, despite regular purchases of new ships from the nationalised shipyards of Italy which never quite seemed to match the requirements of the market. Apart from local services to the Tremiti Islands off the coast north of Ancona the only ships using the Adriatica name are now the *Domiziana* and *Flaminia*, a pair of large but uninspiring ferries chartered from the parent Tirrenia fleet and operating in their livery with the minor addition of Venetian lions to their funnels below their owner's less distinguished badge.

MODERN HIGHWAYS

This wasting away of the pioneer companies was symptomatic of the lack of initiative shown by the companies in the Adriatic ferry market until the mid nineties with even the best funded companies running slow ships on leisurely timetables which regularly allowed whole days and nights in the terminal ports each week even at the height of summer, the owners seemingly unconscious of the amount of capital tied up so unproductively. This contrasted to the ever more efficient operations in Northern Europe where ships would be turned round as rapidly as possible and sailed off on their next voyage as soon after arrival as they could be reloaded.

Into these doldrums came Pericles Panagopoulos, an established Greek ship owner who had previously owned and profitably sold Royal Cruise Lines and who brought a more business-like approach to a market which at the time depended almost entirely on second hand tonnage. Ordering a pair of identical vessels from the then leading yard of Seebeckwerft in Bremerhaven, the maiden voyage of the *Superfast I* from Ancona to Patras

on 1st June 1995 quite literally revolutionised the market, only the Greek ports served remained the same with Igoumenitsa still featuring as the first call on the mainland and the route then continuing to Patras.

Impressive ships with accommodation in their bright red hulls for 1,400 passengers, the same as could be carried by the *Egnatia*, the Superfast pair could carry a large load on their vehicle decks - quoted at 810 cars or 1,850 metres of freight traffic - but it was the name on the hull that really gave away why the company was to lead the transformation in the Adriatic as they could achieve 28 knots and used their speed to achieve 20-hour passages on the Ancona route – almost twice as long as that of the inaugural route from Brindisi. A total of 14 ships have so far operated under the Superfast flag – although the company has been astute in selling its older vessels and adapting its routes to the changing market.

The last 15 years have seen the old order replaced by new vessels operating on the Superfast model with most ships now able to exceed 25 knots and only the older ANEK ships operating from Venice to Patras regularly taking days in port in the busy summer season. Only the relative newcomer Endeavor Lines continues to operate the classic route from Brindisi to Patras with daily departures via Corfu and Igoumenitsa using elderly ex-Japanese tonnage, the Italian port now mainly being used by ferries serving Albania, still only slowly opening to Europe some 20 years after the establishment of a form of democracy.

It is perhaps in Igoumenitsa that the revolution can be seen most clearly. The small town at the end of a mountain track in 1960 is now connected to Turkey by a new six-lane highway which finally opened throughout its length in late 2009. Freight arriving into Igoumenitsa on one of the morning ferry arrivals in 2010 can expect to reach Istanbul by nightfall the same day. This and other new road connections throughout Greece largely funded by grants from the European taxpayer are now good enough to threaten the continuation of ferry services to Patras. The many signs for the new road echo the name both of its ancient predecessor and the pioneer car ferry but few of its users are aware of what has gone into the success of the traffic system that now feeds through the Egnatia Highway.

Igoumenitsa in 2009 with Agoudimos Lines' **Penelope** *(originally the* **European Gateway** *of Townsend Thoresen) unloading as Ventouris'* **Seatrade** *(originally the train ferry* **Svealand***) arrives with freight from Turkey. (John May)*

New titles from Ferry Publications...

Ferry & Cruise Ship Annual 2010 112 pages 280 x 219mm hardback
This second edition of our Ferry & Cruise Annual will be available as from November 2009 and will include features on Holyhead-Dun Laoghaire; Crossing the Adriatic; Small Ferry Scene; the Port of Liverpool; SeaFrance Renoir; the Belgian Ferry Scene; Cruising the Red Sea; Harwich International Cruise Port; and notable cruise ship withdrawals in 2009. Produced in colour.
£22.50 inc P&P within UK *(Overseas orders £24.50)*

Baltic Ferries 128 pages 280 x 219mm hardback
This new title written by Bruce Peter follows the development and history of major ferry operations on the Baltic. Produced in colour with many outstanding photographs of the past and present vessels serving between Sweden, Finland, Estonia, Poland, Denmark and Germany. Now available.
£21.50 inc P&P within UK *(Overseas orders £23.50)*

Camera on the Clyde 120 pages 200 x 206mm hardback
This new title includes a wide selection of unpublished views to date of the Clyde in both colour and black & white. Breathtaking and historical pictures from the lens of A. Ernest Glen.
Written by Ann Glen and Bruce Peter.
£21.50 inc P&P within UK *(Overseas orders £23.50)*

Caledonian MacBrayne – The Fleet 80 pages A5
This revised edition of Caledonian MacBrayne's operations and fleet has now been updated and expanded for publication in December 2009. Richly illustrated with outstanding photography.
£9.80 inc P&P within UK *(Overseas orders £11.80)*

Solent Seaways – Isle of Wight ferries – Wightlink 96 pages A4
This new and expanded version of the history of Wightlink's services to the Isle of Wight, compiled by John Hendy, looks at the history of the Portsmouth-Fishbourne and Lymington-Yarmouth routes together with the introduction of new tonnage on the Lymington service and the new fast ferries from Portsmouth. Illustrated in colour and black & white. Published March 2010.
£18.50 inc P&P within UK *(Overseas orders £20.50)*

Dover–Calais The Short Sea Route 128 pages 280 x 219mm hardback
This new 128 page publication on the history of the Dover-Calais written by John Hendy, covers the history of the most famous ferry crossing in the world and looks in detail at the development and expansion of the ferry operations and the new tonnage which has been introduced since the opening of the tunnel. The book will be richly illustrated with many unpublished views to date in colour and black and white.
£22.50 inc P&P within UK *(Overseas orders £24.50)*

Other books due for publication from Ferry Publications include
Passage to the Northern Isles – Ferry Services to Orkney and Shetland
Weymouth Ferries – The Rise and Fall of the Port
Ferries of Dover – Past & Present
Ferries of Scotland – Past & Present
Harwich-Hook of Holland